*Not flesh of my flesh,
Nor bone of my bone,
But still miraculously my own.
Never forget
For a single minute,
You didn't grow
Under my heart, but in it.*

ROOM for ONE MORE

NYLA BOOTH & ANN SCOTT

LIVING BOOKS
Tyndale House Publishers, Inc.
Wheaton, Illinois

First printing, October 1984

Library of Congress Catalog Card Number 84-51174
ISBN 0-8423-5711-4, paper
Copyright © 1984 by Nyla Booth
All rights reserved
Printed in the United States of America

With deepest love and appreciation to: My dear husband, **ED,** *who always encourages me; my beautiful daughter,* **CATHY;** *my son,* **DAVID;** *my sweet granddaughter,* **SARAH ELIZABETH;** *my sister,* **ROSEMARY;** *and to all of my special friends who helped and prayed for me—and of course, to the* **ONE** *who turned the dream of writing this book into a reality.*

ACKNOWLEDGMENTS

My special thanks to Ann Scott, who touched my life and inspired me with her story.

My appreciation to Rosemary Tuve, Cathy Booth-Issersohn, Glennis McNeal, Gail Denham, and Dorothy Hunter, who read portions of this book while it was in process and gave invaluable insights and suggestions.

Much gratitude to my retired newspaper editor friend Claude Baskett for patiently making corrections.

Deepest thanks to the wonderful and caring staff at Tyndale House Publishers—especially Senior Editor Virginia Muir, who encouraged me from the beginning, and Editor-in-Chief Dr. Wendell Hawley.

CONTENTS

*Foreword by
Laurel Lee* 11

*Foreword by
Ann Scott* 13

*Preface by
Nyla Booth* 15

PART ONE: THE CHILDREN

1 *First in Our Hearts* 21

2 *A New Door Opens* 31

3 *An Oriental Doll* 35

4 *Touched by a Miracle* 47

5 *A Love Story* 61

6 *A Touch of Spring* 67

7 *Three Wonderful Surprises* 75

8 *A Delicate Balance* 83

9 Plan Loving Adoptions Now   93

10 Against Great Odds   103

11 Boy with a Mission   115

12 An Adoption Failure   125

13 Street Boy from Calcutta   139

14 A Dangerous Voyage   153

15 An Enchanted Evening   163

PART TWO: OTHER CHALLENGES

16 House of the Open Door   171

17 "What's for Supper?"   181

18 Love and Blessings   187

19 "Two Days Off for Good Behavior"   193

20 Adoption Days   197

Epilogue: An Update   201

Appendix: Steps in Adopting a Child   207

FOREWORD
"Welcome to a Family"

It would be great if the cover of this book looked like the Scotts' front door. Through the years the home of Phil and Ann Scott has changed from one resembling other houses on their country road to a place renowned for treasure.

The rooms will not be elaborate with furnishings. The riches lie within the remarkable family who inhabits that dwelling and now the pages of this book.

May Christ guide the reader through these passages and underline for you principles of faith and trust. For the lives that are demonstrated in this book exemplify how the gift of Jesus Christ can shine forth with the eternal and real riches of sacrificial love.

Laurel Lee

FOREWORD

I'll never forget the first year of our marriage. It was 1949. Phil bought sixty acres of land in the picturesque Willamette Valley, situated between the farm towns of McMinnville and Sheridan, Oregon. Later we had an opportunity to buy adjacent land, making a total of 114 acres. Its meadows are emerald green, and the wooded hills climb majestically toward the sky.

Phil borrowed $1,000 and bought lumber for the first part of our house. Slowly, by trial and much error, we began to build. Every spare moment was spent building. That whole first year we lived with Phil's patient parents.

Phil worked in a plywood mill, and I was employed in McMinnville as a hairdresser and cosmetologist. Each payday we bought as many boards as we could afford. My saw rippled in and out, creating crooked lines and unexpected scallops. Every muscle ached. In the rainy season, ankle-deep mud surrounded us. But it was fun. We were young and in love. Every little accomplishment seemed major to us.

As soon as we had an exterior shell with a roof on and the inside studded, we moved in. We thought we were living in a palace. What we actually had was a tiny one-bedroom house. Every room was small. The whole house measured twenty by twenty-four feet.

Today the original one-bedroom house has expanded into a home 102 feet long and 51 feet at its widest point. It contains eleven bedrooms and four bathrooms.

We've never used a blueprint, but God must have designed it. He also designed our family of seventeen children from many countries and cultures and filled it with love and beauty.

The story of how we came to build and fill this "house with the open door" is also the story of how God took our grief and turned it into joy. He also sent many lessons for us to learn along the way.

Ann Scott

PREFACE

This is an incredible story of the love and mercy of God and the devotion of his servants Ann Scott and her husband, Phil.

Ann may question, and she might cry, but above all, she is obedient to God—and he blesses her abundantly.

Here is her story, as she related it to me in many meetings over cups of steaming coffee. May it be a blessing and inspiration to all who read it.

Nyla Booth

PART ONE
THE CHILDREN

THE SCOTT FAMILY PORTRAIT

Phyllis: *the beautiful first child of Ann and Phil Scott.*
Cindy: *the second-born child of Ann and Phil—a dream come true.*
Angie: *a blonde, blue-eyed girl—our first adoption (arrived 9/65).*
Marci: *a two-year-old Oriental girl from Korea (arrived 12/67).*
Lisa: *a Scotch-Irish lass from California—in need of a miracle (arrived 6/68).*
Cammi: *a Korean orphan girl who prayed for a mommy and a daddy (arrived 8/69).*

April: a Black-Korean girl with two families (arrived 8/70).

Susan: a shy Korean girl with a creative flair (arrived 6/72).

Joe and Paul: mischievous brothers from Korea who join the all-girl household (arrived 6/73).

Christina: an abused child of American Indian and Dutch extraction (adopted 7/74).

Mark: a severely handicapped boy from Vietnam—a profile of courage (arrived 8/75).

Jeremy: a gentle Vietnamese boy rescued in an unexpected way (arrived 3/77).

Aaron: a boy from India with abnormal fears (arrived 12/79).

Maria: a beautiful South American girl who nearly destroyed the family (adopted 12/79).

James and John: Buddhist boys involved in a daring escape from Vietnam (arrived 8/80).

ONE
First in Our Hearts

It was late spring and the welcome promise of summer hung fragrant. Golden sunlight filtered in through the kitchen window, making dancing patterns on the floor. I stood with my hands deep in hot, sudsy dishwater, but my mind was back fourteen years earlier to another spring heavy with promise.

My young husband, Phil, and I had dreamed then of having a baby. But our dreams were shattered when Phyllis, our first-born, arrived.

"Mr. and Mrs. Scott, I don't know how to say this, but I'm sorry. Your daughter is severely brain-damaged." The doctor's words had hit us like violent blows.

Our beautiful baby severely brain-damaged? How could it be? What had we done wrong? As if the knowledge would have

21

eased the pain. We'd suspected something wasn't right, but this?

Phyllis would cry for hours at a time, night and day. I knew she was in pain. When we first took her to a doctor, he examined her and said, "Your baby is just spoiled. You give her too much attention."

Relatives and acquaintances had babies who rolled over, sat up, crawled, and said, "Da-da." Phyllis didn't do any of these things. Our friends found it hard to understand why Phil and I bragged for days when Phyllis actually picked up a toy—or almost smiled.

We made the rounds of doctors. If we heard of anyone who might be able to help, we gathered up our precious baby and took her. We spent a lot of money in those days looking for hope. One doctor would say that she would soon be normal and our hopes were up. The next doctor would paint such a dismal picture that Phil and I would go home shaken with helplessness and despair.

As time went by, we had to accept the truth. Our beautiful child was severely brain-damaged.

Phyllis had been delivered by forceps, and at first we blamed the doctor for the baby's damage. In our mutual pain Phil and I drew closer to each other. Eventually we came to a crossroad. We could be bitter and destroy our lives in the process, or we could forgive the doctor and go forward. There was only one answer for us. We made a conscious decision to forgive. Our marriage grew stronger as together we turned to God and he comforted our aching hearts.

We devoted our lives to taking care of our baby. I made hand-smocked, ruffled little dresses and combed her shining hair into long curls. I learned how to position her so she didn't have as much pain.

One day as I looked into her bright blue eyes, I thought she couldn't see me. I rushed her to an ophthalmologist. He gave us the devastating news that Phyllis could see only as far as her arm's length, and then only dimly.

Soon after that, the doctors told us she was deaf in both ears. She longed to hear; we got little hearing aids for her. We couldn't tell when they needed adjusting: when they whistled in her ears, she would yank them out.

I would play my great-grandmother's beautiful hand-carved rosewood piano bought over 100 years ago. Phyllis seemed content to sit by the hour with her head laid upon the keyboard, feeling the vibrations. She loved music. We bought a little piano for her, and she would lay her curly head upon some part of it and play on the keys with one hand.

As the years went by, we were very protective of her. I wouldn't leave her with anyone else. I felt Phil and I were the only ones who knew how to take care of her, relieve some of her pain, comfort her.

Phyllis began having more and more seizures, sometimes up to eight a day. We couldn't take her to church or any place. People didn't understand, and were frightened when she had a seizure. Phil and I had no social life.

The year Phyllis turned five, the doctors began to insist that we try to get her into a special institution for mentally and emotionally damaged children and adults. I couldn't bring myself to agree. What made me even consider it was learning that there was a three-year waiting list. Before three years, I believed, there would surely be a new medical cure, or God would heal her.

When a doctor from the institution called in six months to say they had room for her right away, I wasn't prepared emotionally, but we believed it was for the best.

The day came to take Phyllis to the institution. I dressed her carefully in a ruffled blue dress that matched her eyes, combed the brown curls around my fingers, and kissed the soft cheeks. We drove to the institution in silence.

When we arrived an hour later Phil took her in his arms and carried her in. We were met by kind and loving people who welcomed Phyllis, but when I had to say good-bye and turn to walk away, I didn't think I could survive. Taking this beautiful child, who had been a part of us for five years, was like losing a child through death who had never died. We couldn't find a way to finish our grief.

They wouldn't let us visit Phyllis for a month because they wanted her to settle down and to accept her new surroundings. I couldn't wait to see her. When we went, I was shocked to see that her long curls had been cut off, her brown cotton dress was plain. It hurt deeply to realize that she didn't recognize us as mommy and daddy. Seeing her in those surroundings seemed so artificial, so sterile. I cried for days afterward.

It was always the same. I couldn't wait for visiting day, and then I would sob all the way home.

We knew we had to put our lives back together, so I returned to work in a beauty shop to pay for Phyllis's care. That was good—it kept me busy. During that first year Phyllis was away, we went to church, caught up on visiting friends, went to the movies, and even took two fun trips. But thoughts of Phyllis were always in our hearts.

At first we were afraid to try to have another baby. Gradually God's reassuring love gave us the courage to dream of another child, whole and healthy. We were thrilled when I knew I was pregnant again. We hoped God would give us another little girl. As our excitement grew, I woke up nights thinking of girls' names.

We chose a new doctor who came highly recommended. He seemed compassionate, and I felt more confident when he said he wouldn't take any chances. This baby would be born by cesarean section. I had a good report during each visit to the doctor. The baby was growing right on schedule, and I felt well, so I was able to work all during the pregnancy. My salary went to help pay for Phyllis's care at Fairview.

During my eighth-month checkup the doctor suggested that I stop by the hospital on the way home to make the arrangements for the cesarean delivery. I was filled with joy and anticipation. Just four more weeks and we would be holding our new baby!

The very next morning I was preparing Phil's breakfast when I began to have severe stomach cramps. It was too early for the baby to come. Maybe it was the flu. "Phil, I feel terrible. I'm going back to bed for a while," I said, turning to make my way slowly down the hall and into bed. After trying one position and then another, I felt more and more uncomfortable. The pain became more intense. Before I realized it, I was groaning softly. Why had I sent Phil away so quickly? Perhaps after resting a little while I could get up and phone him. A pain grabbed me like a vise.

I felt someone gently take my hand. When I opened my eyes, I saw Phil standing beside the bed. "Ann, honey, let me help you up. I stopped on the way to work and called the doctor. He said to take you to the hospital immediately!"

In the hospital's examining room the doctor's forehead creased in a deep frown. The words fell like thunder: "Mrs. Scott, you are in advanced labor. Your baby is now much too far down in the birth canal for a cesarean delivery."

He motioned for Phil to follow him into the hall and left me with the nurse. He didn't waste words. "Mr. Scott, your wife has a very small pelvic area. There is only one chance in a hundred for a normal delivery. We'll do the best we can."

Phil went to the nearest telephone to ask our friends for immediate prayer.

While I was going through labor, Phil was left to wait anxiously with the unbearable thoughts of what could go wrong. He knew we needed a miracle to save this baby. One by one our friends asked God to guide and protect our precious little one.

It was a perfect delivery. When the doctor came out to give Phil the glad news, he said, "I didn't deliver that baby. It was as if someone else were there guiding and delivering her." In the same breath he pleaded, "Please don't try to have any more."

We named our healthy six-pound baby girl Cynthia Jean and called her Cindy. She was a month early, and the first time I saw her I thought she was almost scrawny. When Phil came in, I exclaimed, "Honey, your baby girl looks just like a plucked chicken!"

He quickly protested, "Oh, no, she's the most beautiful baby who ever lived!"

We were a proud and happy threesome as we came home from the hospital. It was fun to show her off to our visitors. She was perfect in every way. We cherished her all the more as we remembered the doctor's well-meant words to us—"No more babies." She would be our last. We considered Cindy a very special gift from heaven.

As Cindy grew, we felt that every word she said, every step she took was a miracle. It was exciting to see her learning to do so many things. She was bright and quick. Her blue eyes sparkled with vitality. Her exquisite pink-cheeked little face was framed by blonde curls. We enjoyed dressing her in dainty ruffled dresses. As Cindy grew older, we lavished all of our attention on her, as did grandmas, grandpas, aunts, and uncles.

Coming out of my reverie, I looked out the window and saw Cindy playing alone in the back yard. *Phyllis is already fourteen years old, and Cindy is seven.* My heart felt grateful, but then my thoughts took a troubled turn. *Cindy seems so lonely,* I brooded. *No wonder she asks so insistently for a baby sister. And there is nothing we can do.*

At that moment the sun, which had been hidden behind the clouds, came out, filling the room with bright warmth. With it came what I sensed to be God's clear command: "Call an adoption agency in Portland. They have a child for you!"

The suddenness and urgency of those words gripped me. I was so startled I immediately turned to the telephone listing for adoption agencies. With trembling fingers I dialed the number and made an appointment.

Not all of our friends shared my conviction. Some warned, "That agency is very difficult to adopt from, and you are just a farm couple. The agency won't be impressed with those 114 nonproductive acres and Phil's earnings from the plywood mill."

We were waiting the outcome, sensing the Lord's guidance. But just how would he lead? Would we ever get that child I knew he had promised?

TWO
A New Door Opens

Spring gave way to summer, and summer in its turn yielded to fall. The weather turned sharp and bitter, but December's raindrops danced and the skies seemed to glow when we held a seven-month-old, blue-eyed, blonde-haired baby of German-English extraction named Angela. Cindy had a sister! The adoption had taken seven months. The agency had sought a couple who knew "how to parent." They had chosen us for a special reason!

The reason was apparent when we got Angela home. Our perfect baby was a perfect terror! She was a hyperkinetic child. Not only did she cry all the time, but she was nervous and couldn't sleep at night. She could walk, almost run, by the time she was eight months old. In those days, in spite of continued exhaustion, we learned we had to watch her during her every waking moment to keep her from destroying herself—or the house!

Our doctor said Angela's problems were extremely severe, and he kept the growing child on medication. It was difficult—and sometimes impossible—to get the right balance of medication so that Angela would neither "climb the walls" nor subside into a drugged, groggy state.

Why had God sent us such a child? How could we supply her needs when they seemed so relentless, so unending? Even Cynthia felt the strain.

I had always believed that God could heal. We prayed diligently for Angela, whom we began calling Angie.

One day we received an invitation to attend a Christian retreat. Could we come for two days? We both felt a strong desire to go, but didn't have the money to hire a baby-sitter or to stay overnight.

We decided to pack a lunch and stay for part of one day. As we arrived on the flower-bordered grounds, the Lord put these tender words into my mind: "This day Angela will receive her healing!" At the same time he gave me faith to believe that our child would be healed. I felt happy and peaceful as the warm summer sun shone on me. As we entered the lodge and found our seats, the speaker began to talk about healing. *That's perfect,* I thought excitedly. *I know God will heal her!*

I hurried forward after the meeting. "Will you pray for my little girl?" I asked with complete confidence. To my amazement, he refused. "No, I am sorry, but I will pray after the evening meeting."

Deep disappointment flooded my spirit. The day that had begun with such bright promise and hope soon became a terrible one. Angie ran out of medicine, and she was a wild animal, never slowing down or pausing for breath.

By late afternoon Phil said, "I don't care what happens! I'm exhausted and embarrassed. We're leaving now!"

I stood firm. God had given me a promise. I had to stay.

It was a long evening. At last the service ended. Tired and anxious, we again walked forward. I repeated the same question to the speaker: "Will you pray for my little girl?"

The minister sat down and very gently lifted Angie to his lap. "Jesus, please show me what is wrong." His face grew solemn, as if he could see in detail the problem in the little brain. He prayed simply. "Jesus, please remove the damaged portion."

Immediately Angie's head dropped until her chin touched her chest. Her eyes closed. Her breathing changed.

My mind raced. *Wait a minute! This is my child and I love her. I don't want her to die! What's happening?*

The minister's calm voice continued.

"Jesus, please recreate her brain the way it should be."

An angonizing silence followed; then Angie lifted her head and opened her eyes. Phil and I, barely daring to breathe, looked into the eyes that had always shot back a fierce gaze, like that of a tormented creature.

Angie turned toward us, her blue eyes clear and beautiful and filled with love, instead. "Mama, Mama, I saw Jesus! Jesus came to me. I feel so good," she whispered.

The trip home was filled with laughter, tears, rejoicing, and thanking the Lord.

Then came morning. I awoke with a start. My first thoughts were *Angie hasn't had her medicine! The house will be in shambles.* I ran toward her room but stopped abruptly at the door to the living room.

Angie and Cindy were sitting on the couch, quietly sharing a book. Angie's attention was captured entirely by her older sister's voice and the colorful pictures. I caught my breath sharply. Cindy looked up, beaming. "Mom, it really worked! I have a sister I can play with now."

I can never forget that moment. The old Angie was gone—never again did she need medication! The new Angie was the child I had longed for on the sunny spring day when I had heard, then acted on, that urgent command. Praise God! He had given us a truly perfect child!

THREE
An Oriental Doll

Cindy was nine years old and Angie was two when my disturbing dream began again. Every time I closed my eyes, the same scene appeared over and over. I saw hungry, desolate boys and girls with their arms stretched out toward me. Strangely, most of them were Asian.

I began to lose sleep and cry easily. The children's eyes haunted me night and day. When I told Phil what was happening, he said he understood very well. He, too, had been dreaming about hungry, abandoned children.

"Phil, what does God want from us?"

"Ann, we must be patient a little longer. I believe he will show us."

One day the strain had become unbearable. My emotions were raw. I looked up and screamed as loudly as I could, "God, what

35

can I do? I can't save the whole world."

A gentle Voice spoke into my mind with love and compassion: *"No, you cannot save the world, but you can save one child."*

One child. Was that all he wanted? Waves of relief swept over me, like a soothing breeze. Surely we could do that, but I knew nothing about foreign adoptions.

However, I recalled having heard Harry and Bertha Holt speak during a meeting a few years earlier. I remembered their story very well.

Mr. Holt was an ordinary farmer with an extraordinary heart. When he had heard about the thousands of Korean-American children (Amerasians) left by American servicemen and civilians, he flew to Korea to investigate. The circumstances were worse than he had imagined. These children suffered greatly from prejudice and discrimination. Other children would not play with them, since their fathers had deserted them. Often their Korean mothers were unable to raise them. Their future seemed hopeless.

When Harry Holt returned home, he had eight babies and toddlers whom he and his wife immediately adopted. In 1956 the Holts started an adoption agency to meet the needs of homeless Korean children.

I should write to them, I thought. That very moment I sat down and addressed an envelope to Mrs. Bertha Holt, Creswell, Oregon. My note said simply, "Can you tell me anything about foreign adoption?" I added my name and address.

An application from the Holt Adoption Agency came back by return mail. After filling out several other forms, we had a young social worker come to our house to make a home study. She wore a dark gray suit and white gloves. My knees shook and Phil spilled his coffee. She soon put us at ease, however, and we began chatting about ourselves.

Phil is basically shy and quiet, so I hoped she could see how generous and compassionate he is. The case worker carefully recorded Phil's statistics: born in 1923; height 5'8"; weight 130 pounds; dark brown hair and blue eyes.

Phil told her about having grown up with two brothers and two sisters on a 320-acre farm near Wounded Knee, South Dakota. Some of his best friends had been Indian children from the Pine Ridge Indian Reservation.

Phil's dad had raised grain and cattle, so there had always been lots of work to do, but they had also had time for games and fun. His was a close-knit, happy family.

Phil entered the Army in 1943. While he was in the South Pacific, his parents moved to McMinnville, near my parents' farm. When the war was over, he came home to a place he had never seen before.

The case worker turned from Phil to me.

37

"And you, Mrs. Scott. Tell me about your background." I began slowly, explaining that during the Depression years my parents had moved from town to a farm in a beautiful Oregon valley. When we were growing up, my twin sister, older brother, and I had had no idea our family was poor.

Mother had been a school teacher. Borrowing a steady supply of books from the state library, she entertained us in the evenings by reading exciting drama or adventure books to us. My favorite book was *Pollyanna;* I think it has influenced my whole life, because Pollyanna could always find something good about everyone. She certainly had a positive outlook.

An outstanding collection of records played on an old Edison windup phonograph gave us an early love for all types of music. Family unity was further deepened by frequent song sessions around the piano.

My sister, brother, and I played in the hayloft while Daddy milked his cows. We waited by the road for him to return from a day of logging in the woods. We would raid his lunch pail for the cookies he always saved for us.

Summers were wonderful and carefree. We took turns riding Black Beauty, our gentle old horse. There were hills to climb, woods to explore, and a mill pond to swim in.

Sundays found me tucked between my parents and grandparents on a long bench at church. Peppermints appeared from Grandma's purse when I got restless.

I loved going to school in a little two-room schoolhouse. We had a real shock when I reached eighth grade. We were bused to a large school in town. Missing the security of a small school, I stood on the outside of groups and felt country-hickish compared to the sophisticated city kids.

Phil and I met when I was a senior in high school. He had just returned from serving in the South Pacific during World War II. I was thrilled to have the attention of someone who seemed so grown up. He was kind and good, and it wasn't long before I fell in love with him.

Our social worker took notes as Phil and I related our past. She looked through the house and then left. I was glad that after Cindy's birth we had added four bedrooms and a large family room to our house.

Soon after that visit, we received a picture of a little girl from Korea. She was so tiny it was hard to believe she was almost two. She was exquisite. Dark curly hair framed her beautiful face with its wistful smile. The case worker explained that she had been abandoned on the courthouse steps in Seoul when she was about a year old. She asked if we would like to have her. Of course, we wanted her! We were thrilled.

From then on, knowing there was a little girl who needed us, we could hardly endure the waiting. We wanted to get her home and hold her close. It seemed an eternity until we were notified that she would arrive just four days before Christmas.

The evening before we were to drive to the Portland airport to meet our new little daughter, I stood at the window, taking a few minutes to meditate. A soft golden light shimmered on the snow outside, reflecting the warm glow of thankfulness in my heart. "Thank you, Jesus," I whispered.

Looking up at the cold winter sky filled with bright stars, I thought of the star that had guided the Wise Men so long ago. "Guide her safely to us," I prayed silently, then I turned back to the living room. Decorations were everywhere. Our Christmas tree reached the ceiling. It wore gorgeous decorations, many of which had been passed down from our families. Some, Phil and I had bought the first year we were married. A bright angel guarded the top of the tree. Little lights twinkled. Yards and yards of red and green paper chains Cindy had made in school added the finishing touch.

The girls had "helped" me bake dozens of cookies, their spicy aroma blending with the pungent scent of the fir boughs. We had told the children the story of Christmas as we carefully arranged the manger scene on the fireplace mantel. Flames danced in the fireplace; warmth and joy filled every corner of our country home.

Angie and Cindy were wild with anticipation, but we finally got them tucked into bed.

Last drinks of water were given and prayers said.

When it was our own time to turn in, Phil and I were so excited about our new arrival that we could scarcely sleep. Our arms ached to hold her. What would she be like? How would she fit into our family?

At last it was morning. We got up very early so we could get ready and drive to the airport to welcome our new little girl. While eating a hurried breakfast, we switched on the radio.

The news shocked us. "All schools and most businesses in the Portland area are closed today. We will be reading cancellation notices of meetings as the reports come in. There is a travelers' warning. Most roads in the Willamette Valley are coated with ice. Driving is extremely hazardous. We advise that you stay home, unless there is an emergency. Thousands of homes are without electricity because of heavy ice breaking power lines."

"Oh, Phil, what can we do?"

"I don't know. There is no way we can make that long drive with our thin tires."

Just then the telephone rang. It was one of our closest friends. When Phil began to tell him about our problem, our friend interrupted: "Now don't worry. I have new snow tires and chains, and I believe my car can make it. I'll be over to pick you up as soon as I can."

The sixty-mile trip to the airport was beautiful but hazardous. Every tree, bush, and blade of grass had a coat of ice and sparkled in the early morning light.

We held our breath as the car slid around the curves and struggled up the slick hills. The sight of cars that had skidded off the road into other vehicles, trees, and telephone poles warned us of the danger we faced.

The trip took two hours longer than usual, but thankfully we reached the airport just before the plane was due. I rushed to the counter for information. "I am sorry, but that plane is delayed because of mechanical failure," a clerk told me.

Fear gripped me. There is a high coastal range of mountains that airplanes must fly over before they dip down into our valley.

Phil and I held hands and prayed while Angie skipped about, giddy with joy, telling anyone who would listen about her new little sister. Cindy was equally joyful.

Two hours crept by before the big silver plane from Korea circled and landed safely. As the passengers filed wearily into the airport, we could see that the plane had been filled with American businessmen. In the midst of them I recognized Jack Adams, the director of Holt Adoption Agency. He was carrying a tiny Oriental doll with lovely beige skin and dark almond-shaped eyes.

We had sent clothes for her to travel in. For sentimental reasons they were the clothes that Angie had come home in when she was seven months old: a pink dress with matching coat and hat her foster mother had made. In addition to this pink outfit, our new little girl was wearing hand-painted Oriental slippers that curled up at the toes.

We all loved her immediately and thanked God for having brought her to us. Our other daughters were thrilled with their new little sister. Cindy gently hugged her and Angie patted her hands.

Businessmen pressed around us. Having traveled with our little one all the way from Korea, they had grown attached to her during the fifteen-hour flight. One man had tears in his eyes as he took her small hand in his big one and admonished us to take good care of her.

As Phil took her in his arms, she fell into an exhausted sleep. She slept nestled against Phil all the way home. I couldn't take my eyes off her. She was so beautiful, so small. I remembered the births of Phyllis and of Cindy and the thrill of getting Angie. How awestruck Phil and I had been. How helpless they had seemed. Now I felt that same desire to love and nurture this precious little girl.

While we were still in the car, Phil named her Marci after a lovely little girl in the Sunday school class he and I taught together. Our new girl's last name is Suh in Korean. We kept that for her middle name and pronounce it *Sue*.

When we reached home and opened the car doors, Marci woke up terribly frightened.

Phil carried her in while Cindy danced ahead, eager to show Marci her new home.

The house was strange to her. Used to a mat on a bare floor, she was afraid of every room, the carpets, the beds.

I held out my arms to her, but she cried and pushed me away. Apparently she had grown used to American men on her trip here, and she would go to Daddy, but not to me. She definitely did not want a blue-eyed mama!

Phil put her to bed in her new room. After she fell asleep, I lay down beside her. I wanted to be there to comfort her in case she was frightened or disoriented when she woke up.

After a brief nap, her beautiful brown eyes opened, and she saw me. "*Amah! Amah!*" she screamed. *Amah* is Korean for *Mama*, the one who looks after them in the orphanage. Marci sobbed and sobbed. When I tried to comfort her, she put her hands over her eyes to avoid seeing me. I felt as helpless as if I had been trying to stop a rainstorm.

I got up and called the rest of our family together to pray for Marci. Phil began the same prayer we had prayed together for nine months while we waited for her arrival. "Dear Lord," he began, "we ask that you surround her with angels and protect her, and please bring the child here safely."

When we realized that she *was* here safely, our prayers turned to laughter and praise. To think that God could bring a tiny girl all the way from an orphanage in Korea and let her be part of our family!

Although Marci was now two years old, she weighed only seventeen pounds. She wore size six-months clothes and size zero shoes. She had been fed three cups of rice and four glasses of powdered milk each day. In the orphanage, food was very scarce. In order to survive, the children had to learn to protect any food they were given. Now in our home Marci still fiercely guarded every morsel. I would lift her into her high chair and place her meals on the tray. If anyone came near, she would fight like a little tiger.

One afternoon I put apple slices on her high chair tray. Angie bounced up to play. I witnessed the first breakthrough when I saw Marci pick up the slices, one by one, and calmly hand them to Angie.

As the days passed by, Marci became more accustomed to us. The fear began to fade from her eyes. Her posture began to relax. We rejoiced as her smile became more frequent and she slowly began to accept our love. Finally she allowed me to show her some of the affection I longed to give her.

Angie, nine months older, dearly loved Marci. It was beautiful to see the chubby, little, blonde, blue-eyed, pink-cheeked girl mothering her diminutive black-haired sister.

One day I heard giggles and saw the little German-English fair-haired girl and the brown-eyed Korean girl playing peek-a-boo under the table. It spoke to my heart and reminded me that the language of children and love is universal.

"Is she yours?" "How did you get her?" "How can we get a child like her?" Marci was often the center of attention when our family left home. Later, several letters came to us that began, "Because of your little girl, we, too, have applied to adopt a child from a foreign country."

One night as I tucked Marci into bed, she stretched out her arms to me for an extra hug. As she did, I had a mental picture of the face that the Lord had shown me nine months earlier.

This time I knelt to thank him for the miracle. Little did I realize the miracles still waiting to happen.

FOUR
Touched by a Miracle

Marci had been in our home for five months, a time of adjustment for all of us. Now everything was going well. I was busy working at my job as a hairdresser while our baby-sitter looked after the children. Phil and I had our family and we were content.

One day I was thinking about how blessed we were, when the telephone rang. It was a long-distance call from a lady who had moved to California. I barely knew her.

"Ann," the woman began, "a young unmarried girl here in Sacramento is expecting a baby within a week. Her family wants the child to be raised in a Christian home. Would you pray about taking the baby?"

I stood there, too stunned to move. Why had this woman called me?

I certainly was too old to start over with a new baby. God had been good to give us Cindy, Angie, and Marci after the tragic circumstances of Phyllis's birth, but we didn't need any more children. Phil and I were in agreement: we had all the family we could afford and all we could handle.

When Phil came home from work that night, I hugged him and told him about the strange telephone call I had received earlier that day.

Phil has a tender, compassionate heart; even so, I was not prepared when he said, "Ann, this is a human baby, a life. Of course, we'll open our home. Of course, we'll take the baby!"

Take the baby! My heart was not convinced. I needed confirmation from the Lord.

The next Sunday we drove to a beautiful country church we had never visited before. I felt peaceful and relaxed as we sang the old hymns of faith and trust. Concentrating on the sermon, while I still wrestled with my decision, was difficult. If only I knew what God wanted us to do!

As the pastor read from the Bible about Gideon, the words began to thunder in my mind. That was it. If Gideon could put out a fleece, why couldn't I?

I began to pray, "Lord, if it is your will for us to take this child, please have the minister come back and pray with us."

Mine was no easy request. We were sitting in the very last row. It seemed unlikely that the pastor would even see us.

The meeting ended, and the minister came

walking down the aisle. I thought he had come to stand at the door and shake hands with people as they left. When I glanced around, the pastor was directly behind us. Very gently he placed his hand on my head and softly spoke these words: "If you will be obedient to the Lord, your home will be blessed and you will be provided for." With those words a serene assurance swept through my soul.

I could hardly wait to get home and hurry to the telephone. Trembling with eagerness, I dialed the woman in California. "We'll take the baby!" I told her. "And will you please see to the legal details?" She agreed.

A few days later we put our faith and credit cards into action as we packed up our family and turned our little red Volkswagen toward California. We stayed overnight with my sister in Medford, a small town in southern Oregon. While there, we had a family discussion on whether to name the new baby *Lisa* or *Julie.* My sister kept our girls while Phil and I journeyed onward.

We were painfully aware that we had no money for the hospital and medical fees that adoptive parents are expected to pay. We timidly approached the desk in the maternity wing of the hospital and introduced ourselves.

The receptionist greeted us warmly. "Oh, yes, everything is ready. The bill has been paid."

Our hearts were beating quickly as a nurse

led us into the nursery. Which baby would be ours? The nurse stopped in front of a bassinet holding a Scotch-Irish lass with huge blue eyes set in a tiny face. She wiggled a little hand. Immediately, she seemed like our own. Phil bent over her and picked her up. I could hardly wait to wrap her in the soft blankets we had brought with us, scoop her into my arms, and take her home. We named her *Lisa.*

While the nurses were dressing Lisa and pouring formula into baby bottles for her, a young minister came to the hospital. He had taken care of the legal aspect for us and now had all the papers ready for us to sign.

We carried Lisa proudly to the front door while the nurses waved. One or two wiped their eyes. The minister followed us to our car.

"Would you mind if I pray with you before you go?" he asked, putting an arm around Phil's shoulders and taking my hand. Years later, we would learn that the young man was related to the baby. He was her uncle.

He asked God to bless Lisa, committed her to our care, and dedicated her to the Lord. He prayed for wisdom, guidance, and strength for us in raising her. That prayer meant much to us at that moment and later during the stormy months to come.

Lisa weighed only five pounds, and the regular diapers came clear up under her chin. I had to cut our disposable diapers in half. (Phil still affectionately teases her and tells her she was so tiny that he carried her home in his pocket.)

When we reached my sister's home, our girls came running out to pat and kiss and inspect their new baby sister. Angie took one look at her and then hunted all through the car. "Where is the other baby?" she demanded. "You said there would be Lisa and Julie!"

"I want to take her to school and show the other kids," Cindy said. "She's lots cuter than the frog Brian brought in last week."

"Does she drink and wet like my doll?" Angie politely inquired. Marci generously tried to feed her potato chips.

When we finally got home, the excitement really began. Marci, then two and a half, would stand on tiptoe and peer into the bassinet by the hour. Angie, three years old, became a regular mother, running for diapers and holding baby Lisa gently. Cindy had longed for another sister, and Lisa was the answer to her dreams.

Phil's parents thought we were getting too many children. When Grandma Scott came to visit, she cuddled Lisa in her arms. I could tell her heart was melting. "She is so sweet. I am so glad you have Lisa, *but please don't get any more!*" she said.

My dad adored Lisa and called her his "kitten." "You went all those miles for a mite no bigger than this?" he kidded.

We gradually became aware that in spite of our loving care, something was very wrong

51

with Lisa. She was not thriving like a normal baby. We took her from doctor to doctor. They suggested various illnesses, but no one seemed to know what was really wrong. It broke our hearts to see Lisa grow weaker, day by day.

Finally a doctor diagnosed her illness as *celiac-sprue syndrome*. He told us that this is a hereditary childhood disease caused by a lack of certain enzymes in the system. Children with celiac disease have flulike symptoms with stomachaches and a loose, croupy cough. Their resistance to other illnesses is low.

Lisa suffered from a severe allergic reaction to the gluten in wheat, oats, and rye. This meant she could not assimilate many foods, including any containing sodium glutenate and some other preservatives. That ruled out most canned foods, breads, pastry, and so on. She could eat some kinds of meats and freshly cooked or raw vegetables.

I fed Lisa a few teaspoons of food at a time round the clock, but still she was not gaining weight.

A crisis came just before Lisa's first birthday. She had pneumonia. As a specialist carefully examined her, she cried weakly and fretfully. Each cough shook her tiny body and sent shivers of pain through my heart as I helplessly watched. Her red-gold curls were damp with perspiration.

"Mrs. Scott, I'm not going to put your

baby in the hospital. I will prescribe medicine and tell you how to take care of her at home. She is better off with you." I fought down an overwhelming fear.

In the car on the way home, I was grateful for the company of my friend Reva, who had come along to hold the baby in a sitting position. Lisa could breathe better that way.

"Ann," Reva spoke quickly, "I know you believe that people can be healed through prayer. Did you know there is someone in your own town who specifically prays for the sick?"

The thought came, *Why don't we take Lisa now? What do we have to lose?* Lisa was desperately ill and I was frantic with worry.

With Reva directing, I drove up to a small white house with lace curtains in the front windows and rang the doorbell, not knowing what to expect. An older woman with a kind face opened the door and graciously invited us in. After asking us a few questions, she took Lisa in her arms. I was touched by her compassion and immediate response to the needs of my child. I asked her to pray for Lisa.

"Lord Jesus," she began, "would you please show me how to pray for this child?" She continued speaking aloud. "There was a trauma surrounding the birth of this baby. In the name of Jesus, we come against the effects of this trauma. We ask for wholeness for Lisa. Please help her completely, Lord.

Thank you. In Jesus' name. Amen."

The prayer time was over. We thanked the woman and walked back to the car.

I kept looking at Lisa on the way home. Was it possible that her face was less flushed? The moment I reached home, I checked her carefully. The coughing had ceased and her fever was gone. I could see a dramatic change in her. She could breathe easily. By evening, all signs of pneumonia were gone. The Lord's answer to prayer had come more quickly and obviously than I could ever have imagined!

As time went by, I began to notice another improvement in Lisa. She could go longer between feedings. Gradually she was able to retain the food I fed her. I introduced one new food and then another and another.

Lisa was miraculously healed and made whole, and has been ever since. She is our strongest child—so strong, in fact, that when she was fourteen years old, she began asking questions about her birth mother: "Why did my mother give me away? Didn't she like me?" I sighed. Looking at Lisa's sweet, freckled face, I wished I could kiss the doubts away and give her the answers that would satisfy her.

Phil and I had begun taking Lisa to a therapist to help her through her double crisis—the sometimes difficult adjustments of early teen years and her many questions about her birth parents. We learned that not all adopted children and adults have an overwhelming desire to know about their biological parents, but there was a strong longing in Lisa.

Some adopted children want to know who they are—and then who they *really* are. They fantasize—or daydream often—about their birth parents and the circumstances surrounding their having been given up for adoption. The therapist thought Lisa would feel more secure if she could have some answers to her questions and know more about her background.

Throughout the years, I had sent pictures of Lisa to Nancy, the woman who had called me fourteen years ago from California to tell me a baby needed a home. In turn she would write bits of information about Rachel, Lisa's mother: "Rachel has become a Christian and really loves the Lord." "Rachel has married a fine Christian man, and they are active in their church." I was especially thankful when I heard that Rachel had two children of her own.

Through Nancy I could probably contact Rachel, who still did not know who had adopted her baby. Could we afford to take such a risk? Rachel might want to take our beloved daughter away from us—or Lisa, on her own, might choose to live with Rachel.

All one night I prayed and pondered. In the morning I told Phil, "I really believe God wants us to contact Rachel."

"I have the same feeling," he agreed.

When I talked to Nancy about this, she volunteered to call Rachel.

"Ann!" Nancy called back shortly, her voice filled with emotion. "I spoke to Rachel. She could not believe you would initiate a contact with her. These last few months, she has had an utter longing to see her child. She said she would always honor the fact that she had relinquished her baby for adoption and that Lisa is legally your child. Would it be all right if she called you?"

Nancy and I prayed together about it; then I hung up the phone and continued praying. A few moments later Rachel called. Her voice quivered as she introduced herself. "I want so much to see Lisa and meet all of you," she said.

I hesitated. "Rachel, you are welcome to come and visit Lisa—and all of us."

Her next words hit me like a small bombshell. "We are going on vacation next week and would like to spend a weekend with you!" I told her I first needed to discuss this with Lisa and would call her soon.

The next day I took Lisa aside. "Lisa," I began slowly, "I have something very serious to discuss with you. I've been in contact with your birth mother. Her name is Rachel, and she would like to see you."

Lisa's blue eyes got big. "Does she really want to see me?" She jumped up and took my hand. "Mom, please don't worry. I will always love you." She wrapped her slender arms around me and hugged me tightly. "I want to see her, but I'm so afraid. What if she doesn't like me? There are so many things I want to ask her."

That night I lay awake thinking of what I wanted to tell Rachel to try to prepare her. My mind raced in circles. On one hand I owed so much to this woman who had given life to our beautiful Lisa. On the other hand, I wanted to shout, "Lisa is ours! I'm her mother, I'm the one who changed the diapers, fed her, and kissed the skinned knees. I was there through her illnesses—through everything. No one knows her the way I do!"

I prayed again the next morning and then called Rachel. "Lisa is eager to see you," I told her. "We want you and your family to come. We want this to be a meaningful and enjoyable meeting for all of us. . . ."

The next week was like living on top of a volcano, we were all so nervous. Our excitement grew as the day approached for Rachel, her husband, and two children to arrive.

Finally Saturday came. I breathed a quick prayer: "Please, Lord, let this be a good time for Lisa. Let it be meaningful and right. Be with Rachel and direct her thoughts and actions, and Lord, if Lisa wants to call Rachel 'Mother,' it's all right. I can accept it."

They were here! I'll never forget the scene. A beautiful young woman stepped from the car and held out her arms. Lisa stood for a moment trying to brush away a cascade of tears; then she ran into Rachel's waiting arms. Soon they were both crying. Lisa stepped back, she and Rachel searching each other's faces, seeing the same deep blue eyes, the same dimple, the same sweet smile.

I thought, *That is the way Lisa will look when she's older.*

Rachel's husband, Bill, and their two young children joined them. Bill gave Lisa a big friendly hug. "Hi, Lisa, I want you to meet your new brother and sister."

Lisa called to us and we hurried out the door. She proudly introduced her family to Rachel and Bill. I felt drawn to Rachel. She was lovely and so like Lisa it was almost like having another daughter.

After lunch around our big table, I suggested to Lisa that she and Rachel go out to the deck and have some time alone to get acquainted. It was there Lisa was able to ask the questions she had agonized over for a long time.

I later had a chance to talk with Rachel. "Wasn't Lisa a beautiful baby?"

"I never saw her," she replied. "A nurse started to bring her into my room, and I saw only the top of her tiny head. Someone stopped the nurse and she hurried out. Oh, how I wanted to see my baby! Through the years I've tried to imagine what she must be like."

My heart went out to Rachel. She had given birth to a precious baby and all she had seen was a glimpse of her head.

When a child dies, there is a service, and

loving, caring people surround the mother and give her sympathy and comfort. But in a situation like Rachel's, everything is hush-hush.

Later Lisa told me, "Rachel didn't want to give me away. She was just a teen-ager, not much older than I am, when she had me. Her parents looked for a Christian home for me. They wanted me to be loved and cared for. She said she thought about me a lot and always hoped she could meet me. Oh, Mom, she didn't hate me. She didn't just throw me away when I was a baby."

I held Lisa close. No wonder she had had such a strong desire to know why she had been given up for adoption.

Lisa is more secure now, knowing that she has two mothers who love her and pray for her.

We realize our meeting with Rachel could have been different, but we knew the Lord was leading us. We were confident that it would be a beautiful relationship, enriching both families.

Every now and then my mind goes back to that little country church and how I, like Gideon, had put out a fleece and God had answered. The words the pastor had said to us that day would also surely come true. Our home would continue to be blessed and the Lord would always provide for us.

FIVE
A Love Story

The late afternoon sun still warmed the earth, and I welcomed the ten-mile drive home from work. It gave me time to relax after a busy day at work in the beauty shop. Within a few moments I was out of the small town of McMinnville and driving on a narrow country road through rich farm land.

The country air was fragrant and clean. Bright yellow wild mustard and dainty white Queen Anne's lace lined the roadway. Golden wheat ripened in the fields. Fat black and white cows dotted the green meadows. Trees were heavy with ripening apples, pears, and purple plums.

My thoughts turned to Phyllis, our first-born. *Thank you, Lord, for helping me earn money as a hairdresser,* I breathed. Especially since it made possible the loving and necessary care she was receiving in an institution in Salem, our state capital.

I tried not to think of the devastating experience of having had a severely brain-damaged child, but I knew it had drawn Phil and me solidly together, giving us care and concern for others. Together we had made a conscious decision not to let our pain embitter us. That experience of heartbreak was the very one that had brought us close to the Lord.

As I drove along, I suddenly realized something very unusual was happening. I was aware of the Lord's presence filling my car. For the second time in my life, God's words came to me: *"There is another child for you in Korea, and it is imperative that you bring her over."*

I trembled as I pulled the car over to a stop. I sat for a long time pondering the words and trying to compose myself. I had thought our family was complete, but I knew two things. There had to be a really important reason for this Korean child to come, and the child was a girl.

The moment I reached home, I rushed to tell Phil, who was always obedient and responsive to the Lord. He was silent for a moment. Then he spoke the words I knew he would say: "Of course we will bring her over. We must apply immediately to the Holt Agency."

Within his heart, Phil knew this was what God wanted us to do. We didn't have the money to pay the child's way from Korea or the room for her to stay, but God had always provided before.

After nine months of much prayer and red tape, our whole family was waiting at the airport, this time in Eugene, Oregon. I almost panicked when I saw the huge airplane drop from the sky and then roll down the runway. What if she doesn't like us or is afraid of us? This is no baby. She is ten years old. We knew she didn't speak English, and we certainly didn't speak her language.

I began to pray, asking God to help us. Just then a gentleman came up and tapped me on the shoulder. He had dark hair and was neatly dressed in a blue suit, white shirt, and light blue tie. His manner of speaking was very polite and formal.

"I have done extensive business in Korea," he began, "and have traveled there many times. I speak the Korean language. May I be of assistance?"

"We are here to meet our adopted daughter," I replied. "It would be so helpful if you would speak to her, explain some basic things about us, and tell her that we love her."

As we watched breathlessly, the big airplane door slowly opened. We crowded forward. "There she is!" we yelled to each other as a vivacious girl bounded down the steps, followed closely by an escort who had taken care of her during the long flight. She had short black hair with bangs, very slanted eyes, and a delightful, winning smile.

Our helper stepped forward and greeted her warmly, speaking in her native tongue. As he pointed to us, she smiled. After a few moments, they walked back toward us. He introduced her to each of us, one by one. Hugs and laughter abounded. She related well to everyone in our family. The bonding seemed to be instant.

When we turned to thank our kind and gracious interpreter, he had simply vanished. None of us had seen him leave. Could he have been an angel sent just for this special occasion?

After a few days we began to search for an American name for our pretty daughter. A friend suggested the name Camilla. It suited her, especially when we learned the nickname Cammi means "little grasshopper" in the Korean language. That described her bouncy personality perfectly.

Her Korean last name was Choe, pronounced *Chay* (to rhyme with *day*). That became her middle name, and she is now known as Cammi Choe Scott.

Although Cammi spoke no English, she soon took over our hearts and the house. She could not remember ever having lived anywhere except in an orphanage, where she had grown up taking care of babies and children.

She loved to do housework and to help me take care of her little sisters. She fed Lisa and carried her around on her hip or back. After a few months she knew enough English to communicate, and we began to learn more about her.

One summer morning, when she ran into the kitchen to help me prepare breakfast, I hugged her close. "Cammi, I love you very much," I said gently. "I am so happy you are here."

Cammi hugged me back. "Mama, I am glad I am here, too." Then in broken English, she began to tell me her story.

"When I was in the orphanage in Korea, sometimes American soldiers would come. They brought food and pretty balloons, and sometimes toys. More than anything I wanted a mama and daddy in America. I asked everyone if this could be possible. They said, 'No, your eyes are too tip-tilted. In America they have straight eyes, so they might not want you with your "up" eyes.' After that I stopped asking them, but I didn't give up. Every night I knelt by my mat and asked God for a mama and daddy in America."

At that moment I had a glimpse into the heart of God. I saw him in a new dimension, as the caring Father who sees and hears his children as individuals. No wonder he had directed us to bring this child to America. He had heard the prayers of a small Korean girl pleading for a mama and a daddy. What amazing love!

SIX
A Touch of Spring

"Honey, I think the Lord is sending us another child." It took some courage for me to share that with Phil a year after we had adopted Cammi. We now had five little girls in our home and, again, we felt our family was complete. But was it possible there was someone else for us?

Phil's response startled me. "I didn't know how to tell you, Ann, but I've sensed that for about three weeks."

The very next day we had a long-distance telephone call. "This is the Holt Adoption Agency. We have a twelve-year-old Black-Korean girl from Pennsylvania. The case worker there thinks she's retarded, but educable. The family—the Elstons—who brought her from Korea for adoption was not allowed to adopt her since a Pennsylvania agency thinks the parents are too old and don't have the finances needed for a special child. Her name is April."

Because we both knew another child was coming, we answered, "Yes, bring her. When will she come?"

"Tomorrow."

I felt a stab of panic. "Tomorrow!"

We stayed up most of the night, moving furniture and preparing a place for April in Cammi's room. Early the next morning, as we drove to the airport, we prayed: "Lord, don't let us see what people have said about April. Please let us see what you have created."

Phil and I wanted to give her every chance and not reject her before we had an opportunity to see what God could do in her life and ours.

April and her case worker were among the first ones off the airplane. We saw a small, dark-haired, very dejected-looking girl. Her eyes were downcast. Her voice quivered as she greeted us. We did not know it then, but April's mind trembled with questions. Why had she been taken from the Elstons? Was it something she had said or done? She remembered hurting her mother's arm. Was that the reason she had been taken away from the mama and daddy she loved? She had not wanted to leave her home and fly to an unknown family.

As we came to know April, we had questions, too. How could anyone have given up this darling girl? We could see that April had been deeply hurt, but she certainly wasn't retarded.

In the orphanage in Korea, April had taken care of the smaller children who were ill or needed special care. She had a quiet and gentle nature, and became good friends with her new sisters. April worked hard in school, and we were proud of her efforts and accomplishments.

We all dreaded the times when the social worker came to visit. April would cry and run to her room and hide. We would try to coax her to come out. "Please don't let anyone take me away!" she would sob for hours after the visit was over.

After a year passed by, we finalized April's adoption. She was a joy to all of us and we loved her.

Everything seemed to be going well. Phil was working on the night shift. One morning he was at home resting while I was at work. The shrill ringing of the telephone jolted him out of a sound sleep. Groggily he answered the phone. The words he heard left him temporarily speechless.

"I am calling from Pennsylvania. My name is Janetta Elston. Are you the Phil Scott who has our daughter?"

Phil was shocked. April was legally our daughter now. What should he say? He answered cautiously, "We have an adopted girl named April."

The woman broke into sobs. "I need to know how April is getting on. Please, would your wife write to me?"

"Yes, certainly," Phil reassured her gently. As he hung up the phone, he prayed that God would help us to bring comfort and healing to this dear family.

We began to correspond with the Elston family at least twice a year. I sent them pictures of April. I could tell by Janetta's letters that she had never gotten over the grief of losing April. Eventually we told April about our correspondence. We asked the Elstons if they would like to call April on her birthday. This became a happy annual event. We also invited them to spend a vacation with us, but they were unable to accept because of the great distance between Pennsylvania and Oregon.

When April had been with us six years, we received a letter from the Elstons telling us that Mr. Elston had retired and that they would like to move to Oregon. Friends advised us: "Don't let them come. There could be problems. They may try to take April from you."

We felt compelled to say, "Come." We believed the Lord wanted us not only to invite them to come, but to offer them the sanctuary of our home until they could find a place to live.

The Elstons arrived one hot August afternoon. They had driven three thousand miles across the United States. We had them as our guests for three weeks. Having these beautiful people visit was like having Christmas in August that year.

While they were with us, they shared their background and the story of April in their delightful clipped accents.

Janetta Elston, a former school teacher, had come from Scotland. Mr. Elston was English by birth, and had been a printer. They had met and been married in a Christian commune in Paraguay, South America. Years later they left the commune and came to the United States.

After they had settled in Pennsylvania, Janetta began to look for children to adopt. By this time they were in their fifties. They were delighted when they were offered April and another Korean child from an adoption agency. When a case worker came to evaluate them, April was very frightened and threw herself on Mrs. Elston's lap and hid her head. The case worker mistakenly felt that April must be retarded and reported this to the state agency. After testing April, the agency decided the Elstons could not adopt her.

"What if something happened to you?" the case worker demanded. "April would have to go to the state institution or perhaps back to Korea. For her sake, you must let us find younger parents to raise her."

April had been their adored and cherished daughter for a whole year when the case worker took her away. Mrs. Elston thought her heart would break. *If I never do another thing,* she promised herself, *I must be assured that April is in a good home.*

Every day as she drove to her teaching job, she recited the Bible verse, "We know that all things work together for good to them that love God, to them who are the called according to his purpose" (Romans 8:28, *KJV).* Her belief in those words helped that despairing woman survive.

The adoption agency tried to reassure the Elstons by sending letters telling them about our fine family. The agency even sent them some letters of recommendation about us. Even though the agency carefully blacked out all of the names and addresses, one letter mentioned an adopted girl named Cammi. Mrs. Elston remembered that name. She went through copies of *AMKO,* a small newspaper published by parents who had adopted Korean children.

One issue mentioned that the Phil Scotts had adopted a Korean daughter named Cammi. The Elstons followed this clue with a telephone call, and finally with a trip all the way from Pennsylvania to Oregon six years later.

Since then, the Elstons have become established in Oregon and have twelve adopted children, filling their spacious home with welcomed activity.

One evening at a Bible study in our home, we had a lesson on forgiveness. I could tell that Janetta was deeply touched. The next morning she handed me a card she had carried in her purse all these years. Newly written on the card were the words, "I forgive you, Hattie, but it isn't easy," referring to the case worker responsible for April's being taken from her.

Janetta works as interstate coordinator in the same adoption agency that I now work in. We are aunt and uncle to each other's children and a vital part of each other's families. All of this would not have happened if the Elstons hadn't given up April. Certainly all things do work together for good . . . sometimes in mysterious ways.

SEVEN
Three Wonderful Surprises

One night in 1972, I was suddenly awakened from a sound sleep with the thought "Ann, you must write to the adoption agency." As the words came, I knew it was the Lord directing me.

But, Lord, I thought, *another child? You know we already have six! How can we manage more children?* Despite my protests, I got up from bed and went out to my desk. I pulled my robe closer as I shivered in the cool nighttime air. Hesitantly, I wrote the letter and then waited up for Phil. It was almost time for him to come home from work on the night shift.

As soon as I heard his key in the lock, I hurried to tell him what had happened and showed him my letter. Bone-tired, he put his arms around me, and we walked to the couch. Picking up our Bible, he began to read Scripture verses. In that time of sharing, our minds and hearts kept coming back to this passage: "If a brother or a sister is ill-clad and in lack of daily food, and one of you says to them, 'Go in peace, be warmed and filled,' without giving them the things needed for the body, what does it profit? So faith, by itself, if it has no works, is dead" (James 2:15-17).

We both felt that the Lord was underlining these verses for us. The next morning we mailed the letter.

Within a few days I had a telephone call from the Holt Adoption Agency: "Mrs. Scott, we have a little Korean girl, seven years old. Susan has lived with another American family, but they can't keep her any longer. She desperately needs a home. Could you come for her?"

We gathered our girls together—Cindy, Angie, Marci, Lisa, Cammi, and April—and told them about Susan. They danced around us, shouting, "When can we see her? When can we see her?"

Phil and I drove south to an adoption agency in Eugene. There we found a terrified little girl sobbing uncontrollably. We tried to talk to her and comfort her, but she was too frightened to answer. Finally Phil picked her up, and we walked to the car. He sat down with her on his lap, and I went around to sit on the driver's side. We were desperate. Nothing we did seemed to calm her. "Lord, please show us some way to help this little girl," we began to pray out loud.

Phil talked to her softly about the animals on our farm: the three horses, twelve ducks, three milk cows, three baby calves, two fat pigs, three dogs, and two cats.

Cats was the magic word. Little Susan stopped shaking and asked, "Can I have a kitty cat all my own?" When we said, "Yes," her sobs turned to sniffles as she told Phil all about a pretty white kitty that had lived in one of her foster homes.

In Salem we stopped for pizza. When Phil lifted her from the car, Susan put her arms around his neck and gave him a sweet kiss. Our hearts melted. She was our little girl.

When we reached home, Marci was the first to run out and welcome Susan. The two became best friends, reading together, talking together, and going to school together. We called them "The Sorority Sisters."

Sparkly little Susan became the sunshine of our lives. Her tenderness and sweetness made her a family favorite. She held high standards for herself, excelling in everything she did. Her creativity came forth in sewing, cooking, and art.

Often she and Marci would spend hours together writing plays and designing costumes. Susan's favorite costume was a fluffy ballet frou-frou, which she would wear when she entertained us by dancing to records. Looking like a little princess, hands held out and toes pointed, she would pirouette back and forth along our raised fireplace hearth, which served as the perfect platform. (Their sister Angie, the same age, tried to enter their fantasy world, but felt excluded. She, in turn, would find comfort in riding and taking care of her beloved horse, Sunny. To this day riding horseback is still her favorite pastime.)

Tender-hearted, Susan was always cuddling a kitty and feeding it the choicest bits of food. Whenever one of the kittens got sick, she would nurse it back to health.

With all our little girls, our home was filled with giggles, dolls, and tea parties. Phil was greatly outnumbered. We began to tease the case worker, "When are you going to bring us some little boys?"

The next time Susan's case worker came to visit, she asked if we would take a sixteen-year-old Black-Korean girl. Her name was Soon Nan and she would come on a student visa. We spent all of one day working on visa papers and some other documents that would need to be ready. The home study was complete.

But something was wrong. I didn't have the feeling of joy, enthusiasm, and anticipation I usually had when a new child was coming. I kept thinking, *What is the matter?* I prayed, but the unsettled feeling grew heavier and heavier. It seemed as if a big black cloud had settled over us.

I knew what I had to do. The letter I sent to the case worker was the most difficult I have ever written: "I do not have joy or peace. I don't know the reason. Until I have clear direction from the Lord, I cannot go ahead." As soon as the letter was in the mail, my troubled feeling left. The black cloud lifted, letting the sun shine through again.

A week later, the case worker called. "How would you like *two* little boys? They're brothers and have lived with a family in another state for eighteen months, but they're unable to keep them any longer."

"Yes, of course!" I exclaimed, my heart filling with a sense of joy. We were so excited! These would be our first boys! Two at a time was almost too good to be true. Joe was eight and Paul was six.

We eagerly met them at the airport. They were handsome with straight black hair and big smiles. Right from the start, they were *our* boys. As they ran to meet us, they said, "Hi, Mom! Hi, Dad!" and chattered all the way home. They were so much fun, all rough and tumble, the way boys should be. Joe and Paul were the little boys I had always dreamed of having. They were absolutely adorable.

With the boys came a meticulous record of the correspondence between the Holt Adoption Agency and their first adoptive family. These papers revealed the story of their past, telling how well the boys were adjusting.

The boys' lives had previously been filled with rejections. Their birth mother and father had lived together for two years until the father abandoned the family and returned to his legal wife in Seoul, Korea. Trying to support her sons, the birth mother worked in a restaurant and often had to leave the two young children alone. Finally in desperation she traveled to Seoul and gave the boys to their father. He immediately took them to an orphanage, where they lived in a large room with twenty-two other little boys between the ages of four and seven. Two Korean house mothers took care of them.

The American family who took Joe and Paul could not adopt them because of complications in their own family.

A good-bye letter written to the boys was taped in the back of their photo album. It ended with the words: "Now we will part, but we will always remember you. With our love, Mama and Papa."

We felt sad for that couple, but Joe and Paul made us richer by their coming. Our house overflowed now with seven vivacious girls and two lively boys. Life was even more exciting!

One day I took the teen-aged girls shopping for school clothes, and Joe and Paul tagged along. As we were going through the checkout counter, I began to have an uneasy feeling.

"Paul, come here. I need to look in your pockets."

He came slowly, his head down. I pulled out package after package of gum and nail polish! After walking with him to see that he put it all back, I spanked him. When we got home I made him tell Phil. Paul looked up with his enormous dark eyes and whispered, "Papa, I stolded." Phil's heart melted, although he did manage to gently reprimand his new son.

Afterward I realized that I had inadvertently contributed to the gum and nail polish episode. Never having had boys before, I didn't even think that they would be impatient waiting for their teen-aged sisters to try on clothes. I should have given them some money for treats. We never had that particular problem again!

With two mischievous boys, life was different but wonderful. Still, adjusting to the change from an all-girl family to one that held both sisters and brothers was nothing compared to the challenge that awaited us next.

EIGHT
A Delicate Balance

In March of 1974, just after torrential rains, the schools closed for spring vacation. Then the dark clouds opened again and the rain poured down.

A friend, along with her five children, came to spend the week-long vacation with us. Counting them and Cindy, Angie, Marci, Lisa, Cammi, April, Susan, Joe, and Paul, we had a total of fourteen children inside the house every day—bouncing off the walls, either squealing with delight or screaming with tears.

On Friday of that long wet week, a letter came from an adoption agency in San Diego. It told about Christina, a little seven-year-old girl who was developmentally delayed and suffered some physical handicaps. She needed a home. Would we consider adopting her? they asked.

The timing of the letter couldn't have been worse. I was so exhausted I didn't want even to think of another child. I filed the letter in my desk and left it there, while I healed.

One night three weeks later Phil and I were both home for an evening.

"Honey, we *must* make a decision regarding this," Phil announced. Taking my hand in his, he continued. "We need to pray and ask God what he wants us to do."

I rested my head against his shoulder and we prayed, turning it over to the Lord and agreeing that we would do what God wanted us to do.

The next morning, alone in my room, I spoke aloud to the Lord: "You said in the Bible, 'My sheep know my voice.' We truly are your sheep, and I ask to hear from you about this special child."

I reached for the Bible to find comfort in the Psalms. Instead, it fell open to the eighteenth chapter of Matthew. The fifth verse magnified itself before my eyes: "And any of you who welcomes a little child like this because you are mine, is welcoming me and caring for me" *(TLB)*. That verse touched me. If we welcomed this little child, we would be welcoming Jesus into our home.

I shared the verse with Phil as soon as he came home from work. We were in agreement. That evening I wrote a letter to the adoption agency in San Diego. Within a short time they wrote back saying we needed to work through a local agency in Oregon.

I called an adoption agency in Portland and explained that we had very little money, but were interested in adopting a child in San Diego. The social worker I spoke to said she would be most happy to work with us. She went through the entire procedure with us at no charge.

All was approved. Before we knew it, the time came for us to fly to San Diego to pick up our new little girl.

"Phil, how can we go?" I asked. "We have no money for the trip."

"Honey, let's not tell anyone except the Lord," Phil suggested.

"All right," I agreed, wondering where the money would come from.

Soon after, I came home from work at the end of a difficult day and found a blue envelope by the telephone. I tore it open quickly and read: "This money is given to you because of your wonderful love for children." Enclosed was just the right amount needed for our trip down to California and back. (To this day, I still don't know who gave us this gift.)

We found places for each of the children to stay and planned an early morning departure. We awakened to the sound of running water. The toilet had broken in the children's bathroom, flooding that room, plus a bedroom—and the water was advancing mercilessly, looking for the rest of the house!

Phil made a desperate telephone call to a friend who runs a janitorial service and got him out of bed. While we were on our lovely trip, he cleaned up the damage and had repairs made.

Thanking God for his goodness in letting us discover the flood before we left, we joyfully drove to the Portland airport en route to San Diego to meet our new daughter. We were warmly welcomed by the Children's Placement Agency in California, which had sent us some details of Christina's background. She had been born in a New York City tenement, the child of alcoholic parents. Her mother and father had both died of cirrhosis of the liver when Christina was three years old. Then relatives she had lived with had badly abused her. Moving to San Diego, they had taken Christina with them. During the following four years she had gone through seven foster placements that failed. When Christina was four or five years old, she had a fall from a pickup truck and suffered severe brain damage that caused seizures and paralysis of her right arm and leg.

We were not sure what to expect, but when they presented her to us at the agency we saw a lovable little girl of American-Indian and Dutch descent. She had short, wavy brown hair, brown eyes, and a pretty, olive complexion. She related to us immediately, letting us hold her hands, hug her, and talk to her.

We took her to visit the San Diego Zoo and had a delightful time. She exclaimed over the animals, but was more interested in going from one concession stand to the next.

As we rode the overhead zoo tramway, our laughter spilled out and over the sides of the little open car like a waterfall, washing away any doubts or fears. The bright California sun did its share to brighten our hopes. We were falling in love with Christina. She seemed so fragile and helpless.

That night, alone in our hotel room, Phil and I kept saying to each other, "We can't let that helpless child go. Did you see the hurt and agony deep inside? She has to have a change in her life! Christina needs us."

The very next day we signed the papers, picked up Christina, and boarded a plane to fly back to Portland. Christina kept hugging us and nestled close. We didn't know it was the last time she would allow us to feel close to her for a long, long time.

The kids were all home and waiting to run out and greet us. They gave Christina a warm welcome and showed her around the house and yard. Cammi showed her the new batch of baby kittens.

Because Christina had been friendly and affectionate to us in California, Phil and I were not prepared for what happened next. Almost immediately the atmosphere of our home changed. Before, there had been much joy and laughter, but suddenly we had a withdrawn and irritable child in our midst. She fought with the other children. She woke up crying at night from bad dreams. In the daytime, Christina spent hours in a rocking chair, her sullen face turned away from us. She did not answer when we talked to her or tried to cajole her into joining us.

We began to have serious doubts. Had Phil and I made a mistake? Had we somehow misunderstood God? Would she be a handicap or a challenge to us and the rest of the family? With God's help, we determined to meet the needs this little life presented.

Christina was on medication for the seizures she suffered. We consulted with one of our doctors. From him we learned that the two different kinds of medicine she was taking could cause some of the emotional problems she displayed. Her dosage was lowered and she seemed better immediately.

Christina loved our back yard pool where she spent the whole summer swimming. The water therapy increased the strength in her paralyzed leg and arm. By the time school started in the fall, she could walk without dragging her leg. She even had full use of her arm, except for a slight tremor.

We learned that because of Christina's past, which included alcoholic fetal syndrome, death of both parents, the head injury, terrible abuse, and multiple placements and rejections, she had developed a psychological need for abuse. Unconsciously, she was programming people to abuse her.

Her typical behavior pattern is still to make people angry with her; otherwise, she is

usually angry with someone. We have had to
devise ways to live with her anger and not
reciprocate. We have had to wean her away
from physical punishment, and yet let her
know that certain things she does are unacceptable.

The reverse side of her nature is kind and
loving. She longs for approval, comfort, and
love—things we daily try to provide for her.

At times it seems that her mind is like a
picture puzzle with the middle pieces missing. She does not always connect cause and
effect when she does the thing that seems
sensible to her at the moment. If she puts
the hot skillet on the Formica, why should
the Formica be scorched? If she can't find
her socks, why not take someone else's? She
can't understand why her behavior often
angers the other children. She simply feels
that they are "picking on her."

Our best ideas for teaching Christina have
sometimes fallen flat, as we discovered in
"the case of the no-trespassing sign."
Christina would come into my bedroom and
go through my desk, until all the papers were
in total disarray. One day I made a large sign
and taped it to my door: "Do not enter
Mother's room without permission." The
next day the papers were again spread over
the desk top and floor.

"Christina, write ten times on paper, 'I will
not enter Mother's room without permission,' " I told her.

Christina became angry. Instead of ten times, she spelled it out a hundred times, out of spite.

I was busy at my desk when Christina came stomping in, making a dramatic entrance.

"Here's your old paper," she muttered as she threw it on my desk.

"Christina, where are you?" I questioned.

"In your room."

"But what did you write on the paper?"

"*I will not enter your room without permission,*" she read stoutly.

"But where are you now?"

"I just brought the papers into your room."

"But what did you just write?" I asked in amazement.

"I will not. . . ."

The light of realization did not dawn in her mind. I knew there would be few simple solutions for her complex behavior problems.

Today Christina is developing and growing. We try to involve her in lots of sports and in as many activities as we can. She has come the farthest of all our children, but she still has the farthest to go.

At times she lets her sweet, caring spirit break forth. These glimpses of her sensitive nature encourage us, letting us know a beautiful little person is there, just waiting to be released.

We are certainly glad for the Bible verse that tells us: "When we welcomed Christina, we welcomed Jesus." No wonder he gave us that much assurance when he gave us such a difficult child. It has kept us steady and has strengthened us in our ministry to her and to the Lord.

NINE
Plan Loving Adoptions Now

Between the adoption of Christina and the next child, Mark, a friendship would develop that would eventually touch many parts of the globe. Several couples, including Ann and Phil Scott, Norma and Ken Lucas, Ted and Harriet Gahr, and Ed and Mary Miyakawa, would find common ground as adoptive parents of "hard-to-place" children. Out of countless hours of conversation, potluck dinners, and hard work would emerge an unusual adoption agency called PLAN, an acronym for Plan Loving Adoptions Now. It would be the fulfillment of Norma Lucas's dream to help the homeless children of the world.

Cheers reverberated through the Willamette Valley on that cold, windy day in March of 1975. We had just received our official license to become an adoption agency.

It was the first, to our knowledge, made up of a parent group. To think that our efforts of almost three years had culminated in a licensed agency was mind-boggling.

Our neighbor Ted Gahr had labored over the bylaws and articles of incorporation, producing a solid plan of such genius that it seemed inspired of God. Then, after applying to the State of Oregon Children's Division for a license, we had held our breath.

Now we could do more than simply counsel prospective adoptive families or conduct workshops and conferences. We could actually take families through the entire adoption process. We were now in a position to make a lasting impact, for our work would directly involve needy children from various backgrounds and locations.

Some of our first placements were war orphans. Just one month after we had obtained our license, Vietnam fell to the communists. It was reported that South Vietnam had thousands of abandoned waifs, products of the long years of war.

More than forty thousand of these children were total outcasts, the racially mixed offspring abandoned by military and civilian fathers. Some of these children eventually found their way to orphanages, but far too many were caught in the chaos of their war-torn country.

One of the groups PLAN worked with was an agency called Friends of Children of Vietnam (FCVN), headquartered in Colorado. It operated an orphanage in Vietnam, and was one of the groups active at that time in bringing these little ones to the United States. We found loving homes for many of these children in Oregon.

The orphans were being brought out of that collapsing country so slowly. I remember we were worried that the United States wasn't responding quickly to the needs of the children to be airlifted from Vietnam.

Just at that time, a jaunty Chicago Irishman did a very dramatic thing. He was Edward Daly, the fifty-two-year-old president of World Airways and long-time benefactor of orphanages in Vietnam.

Without permission from the United States or Saigon, he took off in a Jumbo Jet from an unlighted runway with the most unusual cargo ever flown out of Vietnam. Nestled in blankets and snuggled up on pillows were fifty-seven orphans, their ages ranging from two months to thirteen years.

The plane was stocked with milk, baby food, and diapers! It resembled a cross between a flying playpen and a picnic area. Twenty adults ran a nonstop food service, handing out bananas, sandwiches, bottles of milk, crackers, and lots of rice splashed with soy sauce.

Between feedings, the adults mustered up a diaper-changing line. The kids played games and colored pictures with crayons.

We were working at the PLAN adoption

agency when we heard the news. I remember thinking, *This is a man after my own heart. He sees a need and responds in the best way he knows.* We were cheering him on. "Come on, Mr. Daly. Get those kids out!" We prayed continually for the safety of the children. Little did we know that one of the boys on that airplane was named Jeremy, or that two years later, this same Jeremy was to come to live in our home and be our son.

This maverick trip sparked an international drive to evacuate hundreds more of the homeless waifs. Nine hundred children were airlifted to the United States that very next week under the auspices of several agencies.

At PLAN, we all volunteered our time. At first I worked on my days off from the beauty shop. Our neighbor Ted Gahr took a year off from farming and managed the agency so it would have a good start. Many others caught the vision and helped.

We put in long hours trying to provide inexpensive service to the families who were willing to take these little ones. We believe that families who want to reach out to homeless children shouldn't have to pay high fees, because they're committing their lives to the children.

Our agency grew very fast—almost faster than we could keep up with. We found that there were large numbers of caring people willing to dedicate their lives to the special needs of "hard-to-place" children.

I remember getting a telephone call from an agency in Chicago, telling me that they had a two-year-old boy with ninety-one medical problems. If a home couldn't be found, he would go to an institution for the rest of his life. A delightful family came forth and adopted him. Now he is a bright, darling little boy with a "forever family." Since then they have successfully adopted several other special needs children.

Phillip was a battered baby left homeless. The abuse he had suffered left him with emotional problems. He was hyperactive, rarely spoke, and once threw seventeen temper tantrums in a single day.

Mike and Evonne adopted him when he was three. Within a week the tantrums vanished. In six months, his vocabulary increased from ten words to several hundred, and his hyperactivity came largely under control. The parents have seen Phillip turn into a responsive, bright-eyed youngster.

After a while I felt the pressure of not being able to do all I wanted in the agency. I loved my job in the beauty shop and volunteered as much time as I could for PLAN. I felt I was being pulled in two directions.

"Lord, how can I respond to all the needs?" I began to pray. Three times the thought came: "How much do you really care?" I thought of all those homeless children, and I knew I had to tell him, "I care with everything within me." With that,

I was able to walk out of the profession I had worked in for twenty-five years. I came to work full-time at PLAN.

When I was asked to assume the directorship of PLAN in 1977, I felt totally inadequate. But I thought of the verse in James that says, "If any of you lack wisdom, let him ask of God, and it shall be given him." With that promise, I accepted.

God has sent us just the right workers—all dedicated and qualified. Now we have nine on the staff (this number varies) and twenty social workers. There is a beautiful spirit of love and caring in the agency. We pray about the issues of the day, a practice that has carried us through many times of crisis.

We have had to "pray in" every penny, but God has never failed us or been late with the money we've needed. And we've presented him with some great challenges!

The happiest time in my job is when a child arrives at the airport to meet his or her new parents. It's so exciting! Some of my staff members and I make the long drive to the Portland airport. There is always a group waiting—the parents, any sisters or brothers, aunts, uncles, grandparents, friends, and other families who have adopted children through PLAN.

At last it's time, and we all line up in front of the ramp and watch the faces of the children getting off the plane. We look for older children with creamy-brown skin and dark eyes or escorts carrying little bundles.

The babies from India come in baskets.

The little ones are placed in their adoptive mother's waiting arms. There are laughter and tears. This is the moment she's waited for. Then it's Daddy's turn to hold the child. Airport personnel, other travelers, and sometimes reporters join the crowd. More tears are wiped away.

After admiring "oohs" and "ahs," giving encouragement, and sharing their intense joy, my staff and I walk out to the cars. On the way home we stop for coffee and talk about every detail. The next morning, at work, we tell everyone how wonderful it all was. We have been richly rewarded, having seen the results of months of hard work, faith, and prayers.

Chris and Julie adopted a baby from Calcutta, India. She is a beauty with curly hair and sparkling dark eyes. Nisha's new father wrote a love letter to her when she was ten months old:

My little Nisha,
I want you to know that God, whom I serve with all my heart, brought you to us, and ordained you to be ours before your mother or I existed. The great longing of my heart to have a daughter was fulfilled in you.

My love for you grows daily. As you grow in your recognition of me, I long for the day when you will sit on my lap, put your arms around me, and call me Daddy.

Few have brought such joy to my heart as you. I pray I will always be a joy to yours as well.

With love, Daddy

Not all our adoptions involve children from other countries. There are 102,000 free and legally available "hard-to-place" children in the United States. The American children we find homes for are mentally or physically handicapped, biracial, black, older, retarded, siblings, or have expensive medical problems. We have books containing pictures and descriptions of these children. Often, prospective parents thumbing through pages suddenly stop and exclaim, "There's the one. That's my child!"

Our agency continues to grow. I've known for a long time that we needed to offer counseling to unwed mothers, provide support housing, and show them alternatives to abortion. We did an assessment and discovered there were vast unmet needs for these services. Recently a staffer, Linda Vollman, wrote up a program which our board and the state board approved. This has now proven to be a successful outreach. Thanks to the generosity of several people, a new addition to our agency has just been completed.

We now have space for private counseling rooms to work with unwed mothers and for a therapist to help troubled teen-agers. There is a conference room for workshops and training sessions, a small lunchroom for our staff, extra office space, and a larger reception area for families.

My daily morning prayer is that God will guide me in directing the agency. It can be disappointing and heartbreaking when something doesn't happen the way I think it should in children's lives. But I have found it the most rewarding work I have ever done.

Phil and I know that our children have had to sacrifice somewhat by not having me home as much as they would like. But they also remember what it was like to be homeless—and they feel rewarded by knowing their sacrifice allows other children to have homes.

Every child, regardless of his or her problems, needs and deserves love. We see marvelous miracles happen when a child and a family find each other.

When demands come, decisions are hard to make, and I'm tired, I remember the time God spoke to me and I know I am where he wants me to be.

TEN
Against Great Odds

One hot summer day an urgent call came from a social worker from the Holt Adoption Agency.

"Ann, can you find a home for a young boy? It may be difficult. Mark is thirteen and Vietnamese. He was airlifted out of Vietnam three months ago, just before the country fell to the communists. He is severely handicapped. His father and mother were killed in an explosion during the war, and he was injured, probably at the same time."

Barbara told me how he had come to be rescued from Saigon. In January a little Scottish nurse, Janet Allen, had found Mark begging on a street in Saigon. He was almost dead from starvation, unable to walk, and he could crawl only on his knees and elbows. She had carried him to a Holt Reception Center where she nursed him carefully and

103

tenderly. She had just begun to teach him some simple self-care skills when it became apparent Saigon would fall.

Janet was certain Mark would be killed if he stayed. With a desperate effort she got him to the airport where they were airlifting children and managed to get him on a plane. But Mark's problems were not over.

"Ann," Barbara continued, "the Holt agency in Oregon is searching for a home for him, but no one wants a child who is so handicapped. He can walk only about three steps before he falls down. He may have some retardation. We can't understand him when he speaks. He's unschooled, spastic, and it's difficult for him to use his arms or hands. But we've got to find a permanent home for him."

"Barbara, we have lots of families who are willing to take a handicapped child," I assured her. "Of course we'll find a home for Mark."

After I hung up, I took a list from the file cabinet. I counted fourteen families who had said they were willing to take a handicapped child. I breathed a quick prayer, and feeling confident, I began to telephone through the list. Many were well-qualified, professional people; some were wealthy. To my bewilderment, they all turned Mark down. Each family centered on his problems, not his potential. Mark was about as far down as he could get; he could do nothing but improve. It seemed to me that he would be a very rewarding child. I felt hurt and more than a little angry. It wasn't fair!

"Lord, why didn't at least one of them want this boy?" I exploded. "I thought you would find a good home for him."

Feeling keen disappointment, I slowly picked up the phone and dialed. It was very difficult calling Barbara back.

"Barb, I've had no success in finding a home for Mark," I told her grimly.

Her answer stunned me. "We really wanted to ask you to take Mark, but we didn't have the nerve."

"What, *me* take the boy? You know our house is already full. That's not possible. I can't. I just can't." I was trembling when I put the phone down.

I drove home that afternoon with my mind in turmoil. We already had ten children, all we could afford and all we could look after. We had never had a child in our home with such enormous physical handicaps. He would need a lot of patience and expensive care. How would the other children accept him? How would he fit in?

Barbara said they couldn't understand his speech. He takes only three steps before he falls down—three steps! How can we manage? Oh, why didn't one of the families on the list take him? But what will happen to Mark if no home can be found? Hasn't he been hurt enough?

"Jesus, what would you do? Jesus, what *should* we do?"

As soon as I reached home, I drew Phil aside into our bedroom, by now the only place in our home where we could talk privately.

Phil, as always, was sympathetic to the needs of a child. "Ann, we must pray about it and do what God wants us to do."

As we began to pray together, I said aloud: "Lord, why would you want us to take this boy when there are so many people who have so much more to offer him? It seems we have such a pittance compared to everyone else."

The Lord put the following thoughts in my mind: *"The rich gave their tithes and offerings and it pleased me, but it was the widow who gave her mite, withholding nothing, who delighted my heart. As you give your all, it enables me to move in and be redemptive."*

I knew then that we could do anything the Lord wanted us to do. My heart and mind were at peace. I shared this with Phil, who agreed. We would take Mark into our home and allow God to love him through us.

I continued praying aloud: "Lord, I am going to ask you for just one thing. So far Mark has had nothing in his life. I am going to ask that you give him your best."

I called Barbara the next morning and told her we would take Mark, but she would have to move fast. In three days we were leaving for a ten-day camping trip to Wyoming. I asked her to bring Mark so he could have at least one night in our home before he left with us on vacation. He would know that he had a permanent bed and wasn't taking on the life of a gypsy traveler!

We talked to the rest of our children and tried to prepare them for Mark. I was proud of them, for each was open to the new brother God was sending. Cindy, in particular, was fiercely protective. "No one had better make fun of my new brother!" she muttered.

In two days Barbara brought Mark to our home. She also brought a big box of Band-Aids and a bottle of Bactine. It didn't take long for us to see why. He was covered with bruises and scrapes from his continual falls. A mere five feet of skin and bones, his body was misshapen and spastic. His features were distorted. None of us could understand his low, guttural sounds.

Mark took one step toward us and fell down on his elbows and knees. The children rushed to him, each eager to help him up again and, in this way, make him feel welcome. They were to have many opportunities to do that in the months to come.

Soon we were all very busy packing camping gear and food for the trip. Two tents, thirteen sleeping bags, duffel bags, food, and a camp stove were stowed in our van—a very tight fit! In fact, "togetherness" took on new meaning on the whole trip. It was a good introduction to Mark's strengths and problems.

He knew very little English, but he was a good sport. We gradually learned to understand some of his garbled speech. His new brothers and sisters worked with him, trying to teach him more English words from the books they had brought along. Since some of our camping was on rough terrain, Mark also learned a lot about walking.

In Laramie, Wyoming, we attended Phil's family reunion. Mark was definitely the hit of the gathering. Within a few hours his ready smile and courage had won almost everyone's admiration. Our ten-day trip was filled with fun, and it gave Mark a special time to get acquainted with his new family.

After our vacation I took Mark to a medical center in Portland for a complete medical checkup. The doctor who examined our new child had recently completed a tour of duty in Vietnam. He explained to me that kids like Mark are called "knee walkers." For the rest of their lives they are usually confined to crawling about on their knees and elbows. The doctor advised a series of operations on Mark's legs. He would need heavy casts on both legs and would be incapacitated for at least six months.

I looked at Mark's thin, twisted body. His arms and legs were covered with bruises, cuts, and scrapes. In his young life he had gone through more horror and hardship than most people ever know. I wanted to gather him into my arms and protect him from any more pain. I knew he needed the chance to stand upright and walk in a normal way, but he couldn't endure more suffering, at least not now. He needed a time of healing from hurts, a time of happiness and peace.

I expressed this to the doctor and asked if Mark could have six months before we proceeded with the operations. He agreed completely and asked us to come back in February.

Mark's time of learning to walk nearly destroyed the house. The first things to be broken were the glass decorations on the coffee table. One day I heard a loud crash and the splintering of glass. I rushed toward the patio door. There lay Mark, half in and half out of the door, surrounded by jagged bits of glass.

"Mark!" I screamed. "Are you hurt?" He shook his head and slowly got to his feet. Mark was determined he would learn to walk.

Another day, there was again the sound of breaking glass. I rushed into the bathroom and found Mark lying on the floor on top of the splintered shower door. This time there were many cuts. I wanted to cry as I gently helped him up and began to apply Band-Aids and comfort.

A few weeks later we discovered that our new dishwasher door was no match for Mark when he fell against it. They both landed with a thud on the floor.

(When Mark breaks or spills something, he usually shows no emotion and acts as if it never happened. He methodically cleans up the area. The most positive thing our family can do is to keep him encouraged and help him clean up.)

I bought thirty-six matching glasses, each costing one dollar. It seemed worth it, because I wanted the table to look lovely at mealtimes. We tried to keep the house looking cheerful and attractive. Since every family member had chores to do, Mark wanted to learn to wash dishes. You might say his efforts were a "smashing" success. Within a month, every one of the new glasses had "slipped away." But how could we be angry when he was trying so hard?

Soon after our visit to the doctor, someone sent movie tickets in the mail. We were to see Corrie ten Boom's magnificent story *The Hiding Place*. The whole family went together, never giving a thought to the war scenes and how they might affect Mark.

When German soldiers came to take the ten Boom family to a concentration camp, Mark broke into deep sobs. We became painfully aware how real the war was to him. All the children sitting around him reached out their arms to comfort and reassure him. Over and over each one whispered, "It's OK now." "We love you." "Nothing like that will ever happen to you again." "We're your family."

We felt terrible about having brought Mark to the movie, but a beautiful thing was to come from that. Mark was able to begin to relive the loss of his parents and the horrors of war in the love and comfort of his new

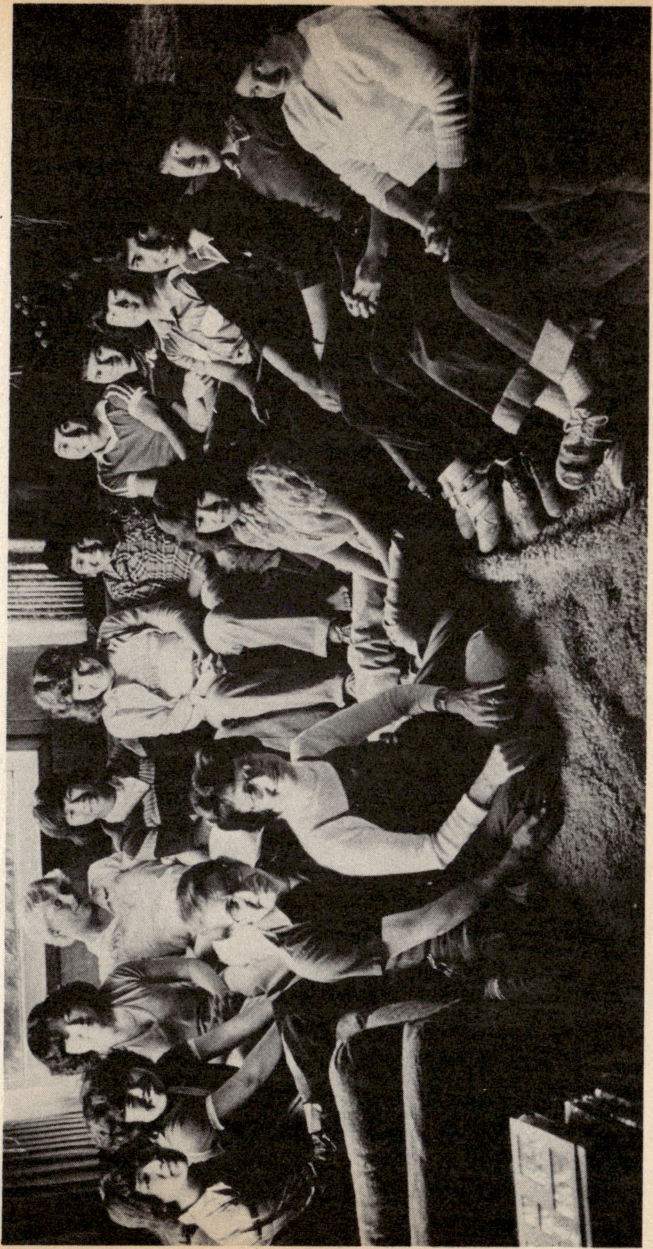

Top left: *A recent photo of Phil and Ann.*
Left: *Phyllis, Ann and Phil's first natural child, at three years.* **Right:** *Phyllis at four years.*

Previous page: *Phil and Ann Scott with their adopted family and a young friend (third from right). Front (left to right): Phil, Ann, and Susan. Back (left to right): Mark, April, Marci, Angie, James, Chris, Aaron, John, Jeremy, Paul, a friend, Joe, and Lisa.*

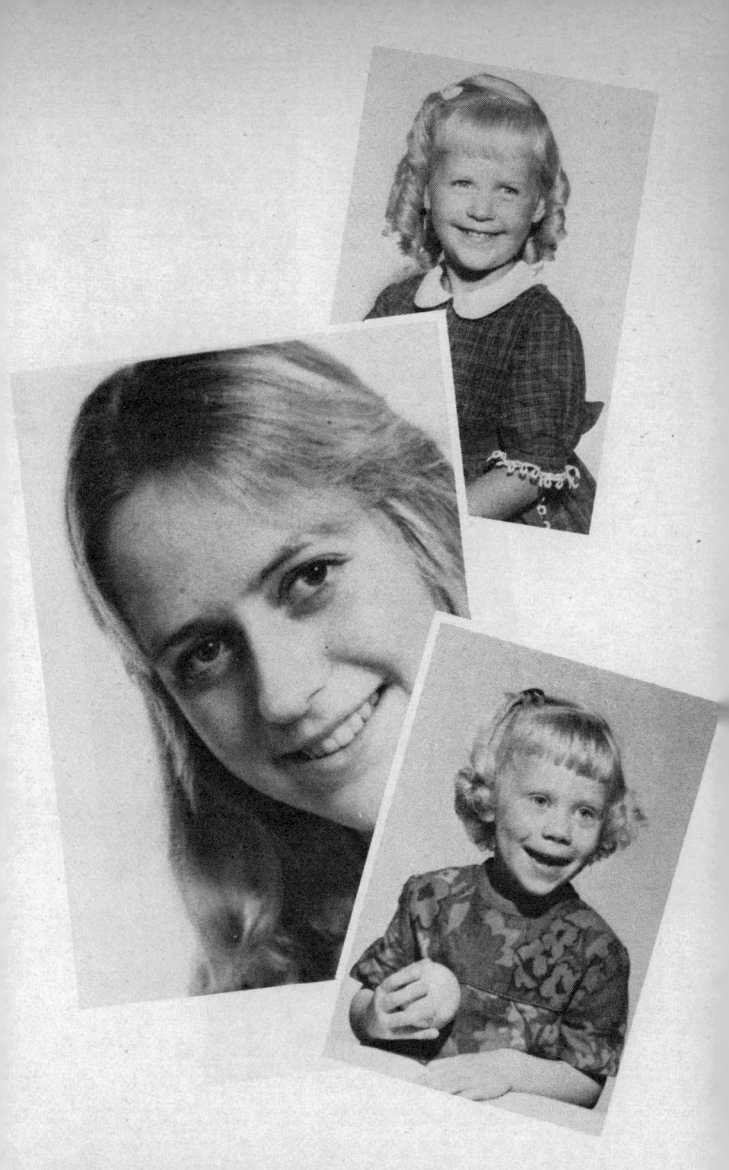

Top right: *Cindy, Ann and Phil's second natural child.*
Left: *Cindy as a high school senior.* **Bottom:** *Angela ("Angie"), a blonde, blue-eyed three year old; the first the Scotts adopted.*

Top left: *Marci at two years, shortly after her arrival from Korea.* **Top right:** *Marci at four years enjoys dressing up.* **Bottom:** *Marci just before her eighteenth birthday.*

Top left: *Lisa, a smiling Scotch-Irish lass from California, at two years.* Top right: *Lisa at her eighth-grade graduation.* Bottom: *Cammi shortly after her arrival from Korea.*

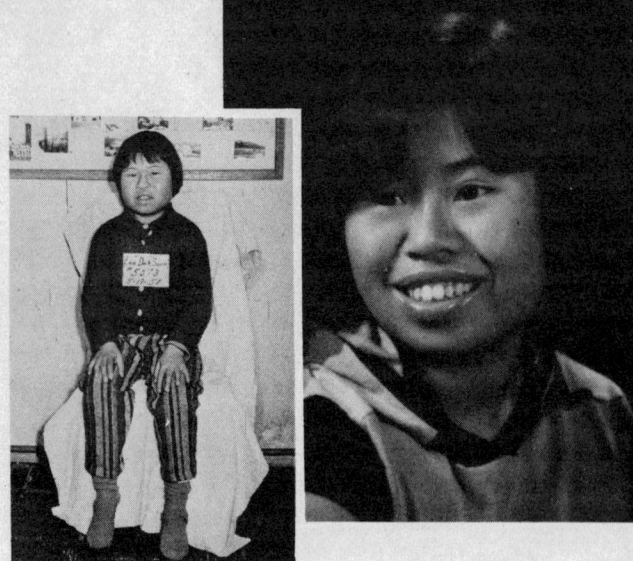

Top left: *Cammi and John, newly pronounced man and wife.* **Top right:** *Cammi and John with their infant daughter, Nicole.* **Bottom left:** *April in a Korean orphanage.* **Bottom right:** *April as a high school senior.*

Top left: *Susan as a young orphan in Korea.* **Top right:** *Seven-year-old Susan when she arrived.* **Middle:** *Susan as a high school senior.*

Top: *Brothers Joe (left) and Paul (right) in their first home prior to their adoption by the Scotts.* **Left:** *A teenaged Paul showing off his sure footing.*
Right: *Joe as a graduating senior.*

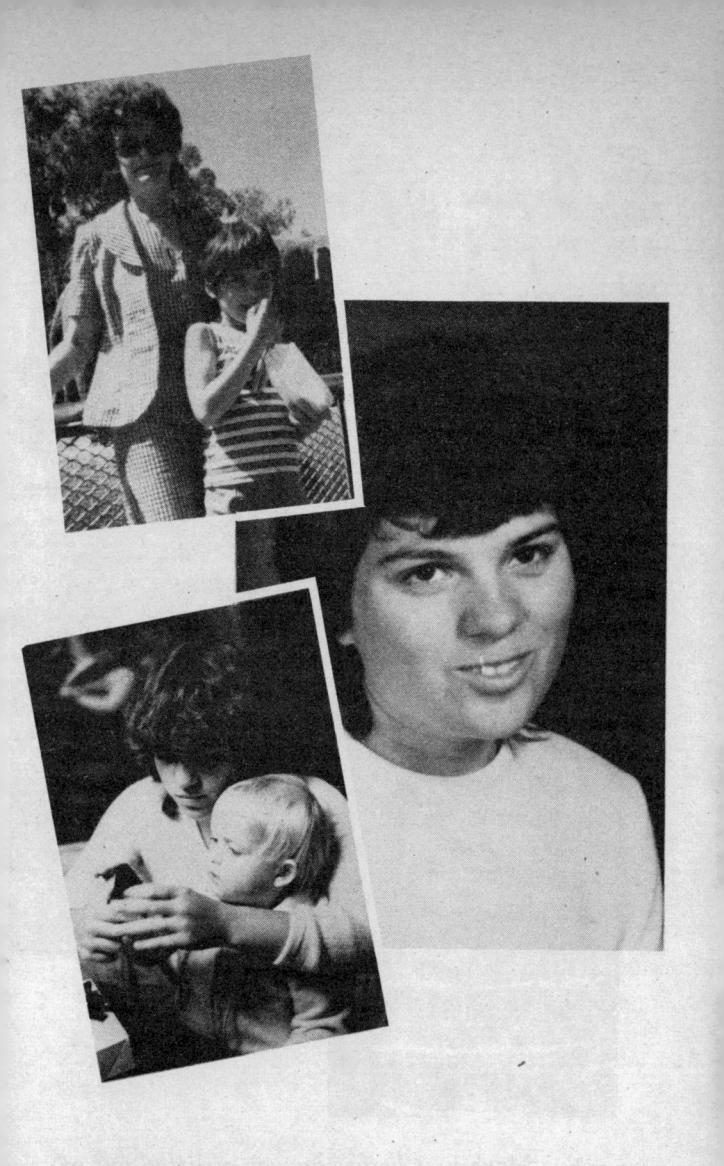

Top: *Christina ("Chris") and Ann on their first day together.* Middle: *Chris now at age seventeen.*
Bottom: *Chris patiently guiding her niece, Stacey.*

Top right: *Mark just before he was airlifted out of Saigon.* **Top left:** *Mark as a glowing high school graduate.* **Bottom right:** *Aaron being hugged by Ann after his arrival from Calcutta.* **Bottom left:** *Aaron beams ever since he found Jesus.*

Top left: *Jeremy as a young boy in Vietnam.* **Top right:** *Jeremy (smallest) with his two brothers, Jeff and Jason, when they were still in Vietnam.*
Bottom left: *Jeremy (front right) with his brothers on his adoption day.* **Bottom right:** *Jeremy at eighteen reflecting upon life.*

Top left: *Maria (right), the girl the Scotts had to finally give up, with James and Ann.* Top right: *Maria and her kitten at the last Christmas she would spend as part of the Scott family.* Bottom: *James (left) with his old friend John from Vietnam.*

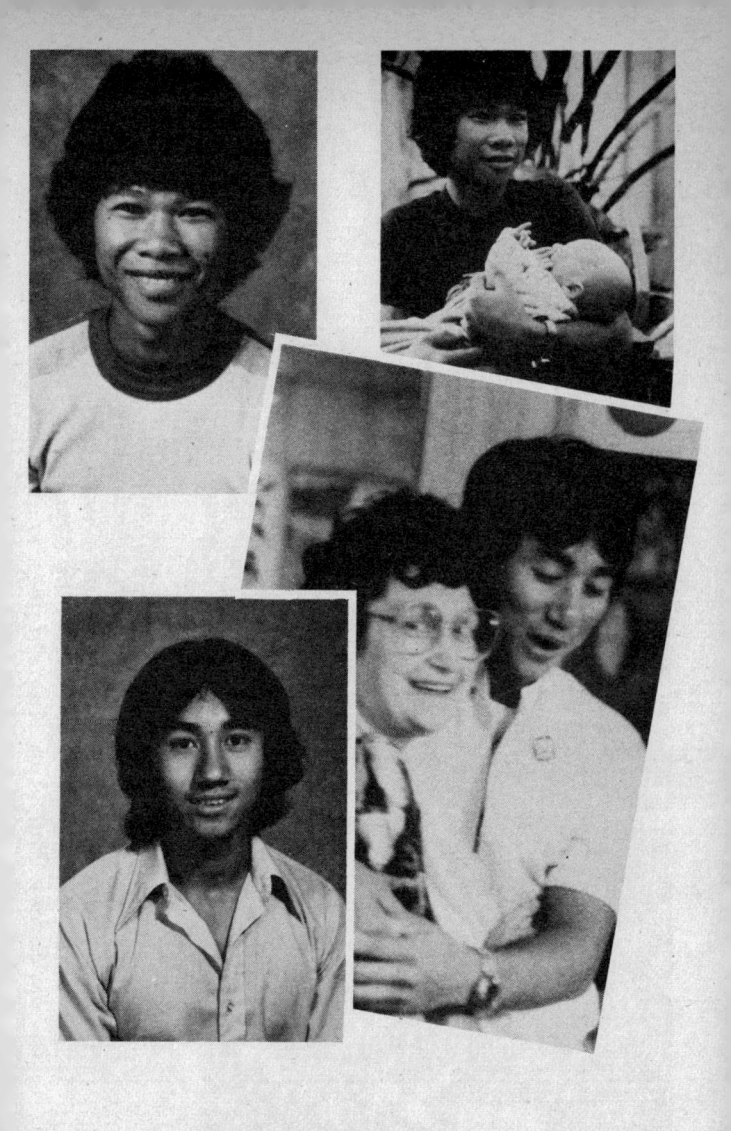

Top left: *James now a "typical" American teenager.*
Top right: *James holding one of his nieces.*
Bottom left: *John, a young Buddhist from Vietnam, finds a loving family and the loving heavenly Father.*
Bottom right: *John and his adoptive mom, Ann.*

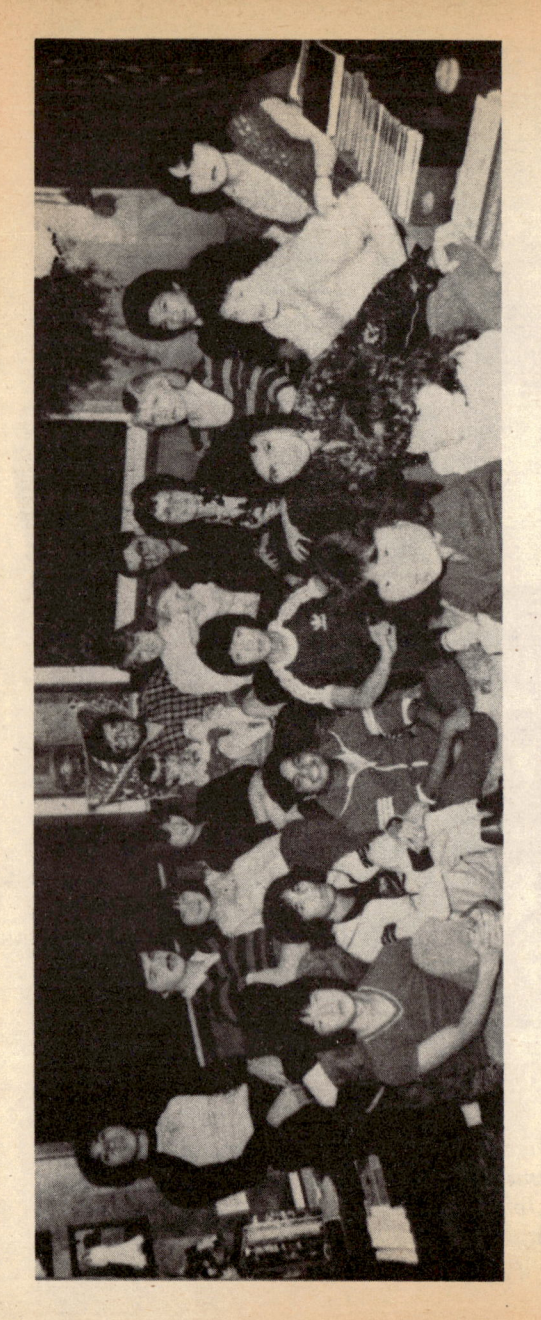

The Scott family, Christmas 1982: (left to right, front row) Paul, Mark, Aaron, Joe, April, Chris, Jeremy, Lisa. (Back row) John, John (Cammi's husband), Cammi, Susan, Charity, Tom (Cindy's husband), Cindy, Stacey, Phil, Ann, Angie, James, and Marci.

family surroundings. God used that situation to do some healing and to take away some of Mark's grief and pain.

After the movie, we stopped for ice cream and called it a celebration of the way God had shaped our family. He had brought us together to love and encourage one another.

That night, snuggled warm in my bed, I felt the tears well up and begin to flow. "Oh, Lord, I'm sorry I was so upset with you for not finding a place for Mark, and angry with those people for not taking him. Even when I was questioning and not understanding, you were answering. You did find the right home for Mark."

In September, after our Wyoming trip, I enrolled Mark in a special education class in school. He is presently learning horticulture and communication. He has an understanding teacher, Mrs. Rossaka, who has experienced war and has empathy for Mark and what he has been through. I'll always be grateful to her. I see, time and again, that God is sending Mark his very best.

On an unseasonably warm, sunny day in February, Mark and I returned to the medical center. The same doctor we had seen in August carefully examined Mark. He had startling news for us.

"Mrs. Scott, there is a dramatic improvement!" He exclaimed. "I no longer recommend surgery for Mark's legs."

The doctor turned to me with tears in his

eyes. "I have seen a miracle," he said softly. "Never before have I seen a 'knee walker' walk!"

To this day, Mark continues to improve. He has gone through dreadful physical damage, but he exhibits few psychological effects. He is a happy, vibrant person, responding well to all that God has provided for him.

Something interesting has happened to Mark's memories of the war. Instead of his dreadful stories about poverty, starvation, and death, he now tells us that his life was wonderful. There was much to eat, and he had a marvelous house. We understand that Mark feels a need to have a better background so he can have a sense of self-worth. (For now, we let him have his fantasies, but I pray that God will nurture and mature him in these areas.)

It is amazing that he has learned to read at the upper third-grade level. Handicapped though he is, the whole world opens up to him when he reads.

The United Cerebral Palsy Clinic in Portland provided him with an electronic communicator. It is a small device, similar to a printing calculator, that can be worn around his neck like a camera or hung from his belt or looped around his arm. When he taps out a word letter by letter, it appears in the display window of the communicator.

In 1979 Mark received a United States

Department of Labor "Outstanding Performance Award." Only nineteen others were honored with that award from among a million participants in a CETA summer program involving the nation's handicapped. It was a proud and exciting time for our whole family.

Mark is an outstanding performer in every way. He has turned out to be one of our easiest adoptions.

Mark continually helps our whole family. How can we complain about the small day-to-day irritations, when Mark has overcome so many physical handicaps—and we have never heard him complain about anything? How can we have self-pity when Mark has had so many things happen to him—and he faces them all with a smile? How can we feel frustrated when it takes Mark thirty minutes to tie his shoes—and he never becomes impatient in the process? How can we feel inadequate or unable to do things, when Mark tries to accomplish everything under the most difficult conditions?

God has taught us a lot through Mark, who has enriched all our lives. The Lord has put a special love in our hearts for Mark. He is still very handicapped by our standards, but he has such a zest for life, a charisma you see in few people.

I reflect back and think of the time when I made those fourteen calls trying to place Mark. I had been so sure God would open one of those homes, the one I thought would be his first choice. Was it our willingness—or our obedience—that allowed God to bless our family? I feel sorry for the families that turned Mark down. They missed a wonderful boy!

ELEVEN
Boy with a Mission

During the Vietnamese airlift in 1975, I had come to know Cheryl Markson, director of an adoption agency called "Friends of Children of Vietnam" in Colorado. One snowy winter day months later, she wrote to tell me about Jeremy, a thirteen-year-old Vietnamese boy.

Jeremy had been rejected from the home in which he had been placed. A broken marriage had terminated his placement. He was now living in a boys' residential center as a ward of the State of Colorado. The state social worker felt a thirteen-year-old boy would be too hard to place successfully, but Cheryl felt otherwise. She saw the deep pain this young boy had already suffered and yearned for him to spend his teen-aged years with a family who would love and care for him.

She knew that Jeremy, a very loving boy, needed a home and a family of his own, so she was determined to try. After all, her best friend, Cherie Clark, had cared for Jeremy in Vietnam for two years, at the same time she was relentlessly working to save scores of other orphan children there.

I pondered over the letter and showed it to Phil. By now, we had Cindy, Angela, Marci, Lisa, Cammi, April, Susan, Joe, Paul, Christina, and Mark. We were content with the large family God had given us. How could we possibly afford another child, especially a teen-ager! The more children we had, the more difficult our lives became and the less money we had.

A few days later I sat at the sewing machine, making a birthday dress for Cindy. I didn't have the money for the pretty flowered material I wanted, and I was struggling to get the zipper in right. "Why, Lord?" I exploded loudly. "Why do we have to scrimp so much and take in so many children? I don't see you asking other people to do this!"

God sweetly spoke in my thoughts: *"I have asked you to have an open door. If it is to be closed, I will close it."*

I could have crawled under the rug in repentance. However, I knew then that if God sent a child, we were to go to the door and say, "Welcome in the name of Jesus." That knowledge, that assurance, removed hours of indecision.

That evening we took Cheryl's letter to read to our church prayer group. The group leader prayed that Phil and I would know what to do. During the prayer, it became very clear to Phil and me that the Lord was sending Jeremy to us—and we were to open our home to him.

When the long winter began to blossom into spring, we had word that Jeremy was coming. We were all ecstatic and went into action. Some of the children and I went to garage sales to find another twin bed and dresser for our soon-to-be family member. Cindy and Cammi pitched in to refinish the worn-looking furniture we had found at a bargain price and hauled home in our van. April made a dark blue and white bedspread and matching curtains.

Jeremy's room waited to welcome him. The children were eager for his arrival. They had been supportive of every new child who had come, because most of them remembered the aching sadness of not having a home.

Finally the time came to pack our whole family into the van to go to meet Jeremy. I don't know how Phil managed to drive with the kids all but jumping up and down in their noisy excitement. At last the car was parked and we paraded into the airport. As we hurried to the right gate, I whispered, "Please, Lord, let us love this new child, and may we understand each other. Help me be a good mother."

"Look!" Joe shouted. "There he is!" No one accompanied Jeremy as he stepped from the huge plane. He looked so lonely and scared. Our hearts warmed to him, and we loved him immediately.

He spoke English well and was easy to understand. As weeks went by, we enjoyed Jeremy's helpfulness and pleasant manners. He excelled in all kinds of sports and eventually joined the soccer team.

Before long, we could see that Jeremy was a perfectionist. He was hard on himself and inadvertently on some of the other children in the family. He had high standards for himself and for the rest of the family. At times it was hard for us to live up to his high ideals.

Cheryl had sent us background information on Jeremy. She told us that Jeremy's father had been killed in the war, and two months later his mother had died in an automobile accident.

A feeling of gratitude welled up in me, and I began to cry as I learned about the bravery of Cherie Clark, a young American nurse in Vietnam. She had found ten-year-old Jeremy and his two older brothers, Jeff and Jason, in a Catholic orphanage. When she received permission to take the three boys into her own home, she gave them a good education in an English school and became a mother to them for almost two years. When Saigon fell to the communists, she knew that if the boys were to have any chance for a better life, she would have to act quickly and get them and other orphans out of Vietnam. She worked quickly to make arrangements.

Cherie drove a van full of children, including Jeremy, Jeff, and Jason through war-damaged streets to the Saigon airport. There they were swept up into a scene of mass hysteria, of desperate people trying to leave Vietnam.

Cherie thought she would go deaf from the noise as she pushed one step at a time through the tumultuous mass, until at last she maneuvered the children to the waiting Jumbo Jet.

Cherie hugged the three brothers, who had become like sons to her. They exchanged quick, but tender good-byes. The young men climbed the steps and turned for a last wave before they disappeared inside.

Cherie sobbed with relief as the huge plane roared down the runway and lifted off the ground. *The boys will be safe now,* she thought. *They're going to America.*

Eventually Cherie was able to save the lives of over one thousand Vietnamese war orphans by setting up a center in Vietnam and caring for the children. She also made legal arrangements for the children to be adopted by families in the United States. Later she and her family of eight children (some adopted) traveled to Calcutta, where she began a similar work at great personal sacrifice. What a tremendous love she has for the children of the world!

When Jeremy came to live in our home, we knew right away that he was a very loving boy with a deep sensitivity to life. He brought a new awareness of beauty into our lives as he called our attention to the crimson sunsets and worked on his knees, planting flowers for all of us to enjoy.

This sensitivity also sometimes caused Jeremy to exclude himself from interaction with the other children. I knew he needed to be alone, to sort out the events of his life in Vietnam and here. At times like these, my heart ached for him.

At five o'clock one afternoon, I knocked on his door. There was no answer. I opened the door and noticed he had already gone to bed. I tried to talk to him, but he stared at the ceiling and didn't answer. Tears stung my eyes as I walked away. *He has to have comfort*, I thought. *Lord, help him soon.*

My heart was heavy when I met with our prayer group that evening. I asked them especially to pray for Jeremy and for his hurts to be healed. Sensing how important this request was, each one promised to pray diligently for Jeremy.

The next evening he came to my room. Sitting on the edge of my bed, he shared. "Mom, I had a dream last night. I was in Vietnam and my mother disappeared, then my father, and later my two brothers. I looked and looked for them, but I couldn't find them. I was so lonely, so scared. Then I was here, and you and Dad disappeared. I was so lonely, so scared."

Wanting to comfort him, I sat down in my big old rocking chair and held out my arms. He hesitated, and then, like a small child, climbed onto my lap where I held him and sang little songs to soothe him.

"Jeremy," I said softly, "you will not lose us. You belong to us and we belong to you. You are safe in our family. God loves you and we love you. In the Bible, Jesus promises that he will never leave you." I held Jeremy for a long time. In those moments I knew that God would keep his promise.

When I heard that Jeremy's two brothers were still in Colorado, my love for Jeremy led me to contact the agency and ask if we could have all three boys.

I was stunned when I read their answer: "No, that would not be possible." It broke my heart. These boys had lost so much. I could not bear for them to lose each other.

"Lord, I know you have a Father's heart," I began to pray. "I want to ask you for one big special favor. Please bring the other two boys to Oregon." At least that way, they could see each other often.

Right after that, God began to answer my prayer. Within a few weeks, our adoption agency had a letter from Cheryl Markson, asking if we could place the next older boy, Jeff.

Our neighbors Ted and Harriet Gahr lived just three miles down the valley from us. As soon as they heard about Jeff, they wanted him to join their family and welcomed him.

That left one brother, so I kept praying. Soon there was contact from CFVN about Jason, the oldest son. Neighbors Judy and

Ron Harp, who also lived three miles from us, wanted Jason. Our joy was complete! God had brought these three brothers together in such a miraculous way! Now the boys have the best of three families—and each other.

Jeremy has been with us five years now. Last summer he felt God's call on his life to do mission work through Teen Missions. It is an outreach designed to give young people a chance to serve the Lord by either building badly needed buildings or witnessing in various parts of the world. Kids have to raise their own money, just as regular missionaries do. They must commit their whole summer vacation to the outreach.

Jeremy sent for material on Teen Mission and shared it with all of us. The reality hit Jeremy hard. "Oh, no, now I'll have to lose my job and not have money for a car [a teenager's dream]. I'll have to leave all my friends for the summer. I won't even make money for school clothes."

He was really agonizing. After a while I said, "Jeremy, if these things are so important in your life, why are you going into missionary work?"

He looked up. "Because, Mom, there is something stronger in me that says to go." I knew then that God had spoken to him.

Jeremy only had three weeks to raise $2,200 for his mission trip. He began to share his plans and needs in church groups. He said God had been so good to him by bringing him out from under communist rule where he might have had to serve in a communist army, or where he might have been killed. God had brought him into a free country and given him a mom and a dad. He wanted to show God how grateful he was by reaching out to help others.

People responded in beautiful ways. In three weeks forty people gave money to help him, and he had exactly the amount he needed.

That summer Jeremy and thirty other teenagers helped build a much-needed medical center for Mennonite missionaries in a community of 900 people in LaCapilla, Mexico, located near Mexico City.

One day while he was gone, a family telephoned us from a Bible school in Oklahoma. They had heard that Jeremy would not be able to work during the summer to earn money for a car. They had a car for Jeremy. It arrived in time to be a marvelous welcome-home gift from the Lord with love to Jeremy.

TWELVE
An Adoption Failure

It was a blue, crimson, and gold fall day. Our family had just returned home from a long hike through the woods behind our house. Laughing and rosy cheeked, we trooped in to make hot chocolate. Phil started a crackling fire in the fireplace.

When Jeremy brought in the mail, my attention was caught by a foreign stamp on one of the envelopes. The postmark was from Colombia, South America, dated September 20, 1979. That was just three months before Aaron, our next child, would arrive from India.

I tore open the envelope and began to read a letter that would greatly change all of our lives:

Dear Mr. and Mrs. Scott:
One of the nuns in a local Catholic orphanage has urged me to find a home for

one of their girls, Maria. This is a small orphanage, always run without enough money for all the necessities of the children's lives. It is overcrowded, and the children must leave as soon as they turn thirteen. Any hope for the future of the girls is dim. Most of them find work as servants for many years—or they are caught up into teen-aged prostitution.

Maria will soon be thirteen. She is a sweet, docile child who needs lots of love. Please, won't you take her?

While we were deciding what to do, a friend invited me to her lovely home for lunch. After Quiche Lorraine and fresh fruit salad, we lingered over hot tea and rolled lace cookies. She began to question me about why Phil and I had taken so many youngsters into our home.

I opened the folder of family pictures I had brought with me to show her. I thought, *Lord, you are so good. There isn't one of these precious children we could do without. Each one is a part of our life, part of us.*

I told my friend about the marvelous ways God had chosen to heal Angie and Lisa. I mentioned the rewards we have in seeing our children grow and mature. "Phil and I believe that when we are obedient to the Lord in giving a loving home to the children he brings, he blesses us abundantly. More than anything else in this world, we want to be obedient to him."

During the drive home I thought about Maria. We had lots of love to give her, but not much money. In fact, we didn't have any of the $500 needed to bring her here. We had already spent our savings to bring Aaron.

A week later another friend who was aware of the needs of the Colombian children felt directed by the Lord to give us a check for $500—the exact amount we needed for Maria. My heart skipped a beat. Her obedience to the Lord was a confirmation to us that the Lord wanted Maria to come to the United States.

So we proceeded with the paper work, and the adoption was completed in South America before Maria's arrival.

We wrote several letters to Maria, but we never had an answer. *Soon she will be with us and all will be well,* we assured each other.

Less than three months later Aaron arrived. He had barely joined our family when it was time to return to the airport to meet Maria.

She stood out from the other passengers with her large expressive brown eyes, delicate olive complexion, lovely features, and slender build. Even though her black hair was cut in the typically short orphanage hairstyle, it still fell into graceful waves. She shivered in her thin jacket and blue cotton dress. We tried to make her feel welcome to her new family and new country.

Maria kept picking up strands of her hair and twisting them nervously through her slim brown fingers. Her nails were bitten to the quick. Her dark eyes expressed fear.

Every child we had welcomed into our home had become a loving member of our family. I had no idea that this time our very existence as a family would be threatened.

Maria's adjustment was a difficult time for all of us. We reminded each other that she did not know what it was like to live in a family situation; after all, she had known only an institutional environment, a financially poor one at that. She was also entering the trauma of the teen years. It soon became evident that we had an exceptionally strong-willed child on our hands—one who wanted to rule over us and the other children.

One day Lisa exploded when I scolded her. "All you care about anymore is Maria. You don't care about us! She hit me today, right in the stomach. She said she would hit me harder if I told you."

"That's right, Mom," Christina joined in. "You don't know what it's like when you aren't here. She keeps hitting Lisa, Aaron, and me if we don't let her have her way. We've been too scared to tell you. She said she would really beat us if we told."

When I tried to put my arm around Lisa to comfort her, she jerked away from me and ran crying to her room.

Maria's disposition was as unpredictable as April weather. One moment she was sweet and sunny. But if one of her new sisters or brothers crossed her, she would angrily toss her dark hair, her eyes flashing, and begin wildly hitting and yelling. Then she would sink into a glowering, sullen mood until her cloud of oppression lifted. Afterward she would act as if nothing had ever happened.

"Maria," we told her over and over, "your hands are made for helping, not hitting."

This became a real problem to us. Phil and I had had years of family and professional experience in dealing with emotionally disturbed and handicapped children. I had spoken to groups and had taught seminars in a wide area, but nothing, seemingly, had prepared us to deal with Maria. Phil and I are both soft-spoken people. Somehow we had never developed the right technique to work successfully with this one small girl.

We enrolled Maria in a Catholic school, because we felt the sisters would be better equipped to deal with her problems. They set to work and prepared a special program for her. Unfortunately Maria displayed the same characteristics in school as she did at home. It wasn't long before her teacher called me in for a conference.

I trudged down the hall to Maria's classroom. Dreading what I might hear, I opened the door slowly. I wished I didn't have to go in.

Maria's teacher spoke without any opening formalities. Her voice had a desperate edge. "Mrs. Scott, we just don't know what to do. Sometimes Maria does well, but when she becomes willful, she is unteachable. She yells angrily and disrupts the whole class. We are all suffering because of her."

My heart was heavy as I got into the car and drove home. We had tried everything we could think of to help her.

One day a friend told me the Trappist abbey might have a Spanish-speaking priest who could counsel Maria. The abbey was less than a half hour's drive from our home. I felt a surge of real hope. Maria had been raised in a Catholic orphanage. I hurried to telephone the abbey and make an appointment.

On the following Monday afternoon I drove down a winding country road past farms and fields. The monastery was nestled in the foothills two miles off the main road. I passed a small lake and hiking trails on the way to the main lodge. The modern buildings were one-story high and painted green.

As I left the car and walked toward the lodge, I was struck by the quiet atmosphere, the air of peace. I stopped to collect my thoughts. Immediately a young man in a long white robe opened the door. "Mrs. Scott? We've been expecting you. I am Brother Martin. Won't you come in?"

I stepped into a long hall. He led me past a library into a reception room with a wooden table and comfortable chairs. His eyes were filled with kindness as he looked at me and asked, "How can we help you?"

My answer came out in a rush. I poured out the whole story of our family, especially the trouble we were having with Maria.

Then he briefly excused himself. He returned with several white-robed men, all wanting to hear about our family.

Before I left, Brother Martin gave me the telephone number of a Spanish-speaking priest who counsels Latin Americans in a nearby town. I felt light-hearted and encouraged as I walked to the car.

The Brothers were so kind and caring. We began to take the children and go to Sunday service or to visit on special holidays about once a month. Our children still love to go there—especially the ones with a Catholic background.

I cannot doubt God's hand in our involvement with the monastery. By now, the Brothers are like our extended family and we are their special family.

On one of our visits I shared with them the story of the PLAN adoption agency and the work we do in finding homes for the "hard-to-place" children.

Father Paschal came to my office a short time later. His heart was immediately touched by the work we were doing and by the needs of the children. He offered his help to obtain funding to expand our program. Since then, his grant-writing experience has been invaluable to us, for it has enabled us to help many more children than we could have otherwise. To this day he continues to help us in many ways.

Meanwhile, our problems with Maria continued. We contacted the Spanish-speaking priest and were thankful when he said he would talk to her. He was a large, formidable-looking man. He counseled her at length over a period of time and really did his best to help. But he, too, threw up his hands and announced, "Maria is too stubborn. She doesn't want to be helped. She should go back to Columbia!"

Phil and I looked at each other. Now what could we do?

To make matters worse, people who really didn't know Maria would look at the beautiful girl with her big dark, innocent eyes and sweet smile and say, "This poor child. Other people don't know how to work with her, but I am sure that I could. If I could counsel her, she would be fine in no time." These well-meaning people sometimes did more harm than good.

Meanwhile, living with Maria continued to be like a walk through a mine field. We never knew when she would explode, leaving us hurt and bleeding. Her outbursts were devastating, especially to our soft-spoken Oriental children.

Phil and I felt as if we all needed to get away for a little vacation. On the first Saturday in July, we piled into the van, and in an hour and a half we were at the Coast. The kids romped and played games in the sun-warmed sand or waded in the surf. The fresh air was exhilarating.

In the early evening, Paul and Jeremy

gathered driftwood and built a roaring fire while the other children played ball. After the flames died down a bit, we roasted hot dogs and marshmallows, munched on potato chips and oatmeal cookies, and enjoyed the chocolate and applesauce spice cakes that April and Cammi had made. Just as we finished our feast, the golden sun slipped silently into a calm blue sea, leaving the western sky painted a flaming red and orange.

The sunset had faded, and the first evening stars were out as we walked to the snug log cabin lent to us by friends. We were lulled to sleep by the sound of the surging waves and wakened in the morning by the squawking of hungry sea gulls.

Phil and I smiled at each other during breakfast. Everyone seemed happy and relaxed. Then when we were packing on Sunday to go home, Maria had a flare-up. She and Lisa got into a brief fight. Maria pushed Lisa down, and Lisa retaliated by scratching Maria's face. Phil and I broke up the fight immediately, calmed the girls down, and reprimanded them both. Maria had the beginning of a bruise and three scratches to show for the tussle with her sister.

When the two girls returned to their summer school classes that Monday, the teacher took one look at Maria's face and called the principal. Without contacting us or asking for any additional information, the teacher and the principal assumed the worse and called a state child-care agency (Protective Services for Children).

A social worker informed us that an investigative meeting had been set up and we were to be there. Maria, Lisa, Phil, and I attended. While Maria was questioned for an hour and a half with the aid of a Spanish-speaking interpreter, the three of us were kept waiting in another room.

Finally, we were told that the district attorney's office had been contacted. Lisa, aged eleven, could be charged with criminal assault. Lisa, so much smaller and younger than Maria, was never given a chance to answer questions or explain.

What had started as a childish fight exploded into a situation where we were warned strongly that it was our duty to protect Maria from further "assaults." The agency worker also told us we would be under surveillance for child abuse. Phil and I were horrified and heartsick. Everything went downhill from that point. If we tried to give Maria the discipline she so desperately needed, she would scream, "I'll call the child-care agency."

Lisa began to wake up at night, terrified. She feared the footsteps of someone who would "take her away" for scratching her sister's face. During the day, she ate little.

Anxiety was like a spider spinning webs of fear that threatened to entangle all of us. We saw no improvement as the months slowly dragged by. December's dark clouds accentuated the darkness we felt in our home.

One Saturday a frightening event took place that forced us to make a decision. Our whole family visited a large shopping center. Phil and I had long Christmas lists, so we told the children to meet us in two hours. They promised to meet us in the van, then rushed away excitedly to see the Christmas decorations. Phil and I bought lots of gifts and got caught in a long checkout line.

By the time we reached the van, we were ten minutes later than we'd planned. My heart nearly stopped when I realized what was happening. Phil ran ahead and tore open the door. The children had assigned seats in the van. Maria had decided she wanted to sit in John's place instead of her own. A heated argument followed. Grabbing an empty pop bottle, she broke the bottom off, and was trying to hit John with it. The kids were screaming. With a desperate effort, Phil wrenched the bottle from her grasp.

We knew the situation had become too dangerous for all of us, including Maria. As soon as we reached home, Phil and I went into our room to kneel and pray, "Father, please give us direction in our decision. We can't go on this way."

Phil put his arm around me and pulled me close. I began to cry softly. "Ann," he said, "we have to think of what would be best for Maria."

"And for our whole family—if we are even

to survive as a family," I added, wiping my eyes. "Maria has been in our home for a year. I can't help but think of it as a year of heartbreak. For the first time I feel that we are failing as parents."

Phil and I talked for a long time that night. One thing was clear. We could not deal with someone like Maria. We were not helping her. Yet Maria was getting all our attention while the other children were just surviving. They needed us, too.

That night we made a decision. Maria would need to be sent to another family—one with the skills needed to help her. The family we thought was right for her took her willingly, but after two weeks they placed her under the care of the children's service division. Maria went into a shelter home—and then a series of shelter homes. When none of them worked out, they decided to fly her back to Colombia if we would pay the $600 it would now cost. We were asked to send her back to the very situation we had hoped to save her from.

Had our prayers for this child gone unanswered? Had her coming to our family been a mere coincidence? Our minds were in a turmoil.

Then a friend told us she was going to South America and would be glad to escort Maria to Columbia for us. At the airport, we put our arms around Maria to pray for her and tell her good-bye. She clung to us and didn't want to leave. Our hearts ached.

Within a few hours I had a surprise phone call from my friend. "Ann, I went to the restroom when we changed planes in Los Angeles. When I came out, Maria was gone! I've had her paged and looked everywhere. I'm sorry. I've lost Maria!"

Two days later Maria was on our doorstep. She begged to stay, but even though we loved her, the memories of her destructive force were too strong in our minds. We made arrangements for her to be admitted to an evaluation center in Salem. There a marvelous thing happened. She was matched to the perfect family for her. Her new parents are both school teachers and totally committed to helping children. Neither has ever given up on a young person. Each child is trained to work, and each one has to abide by family rules. They all live together in a large, beautiful home with parklike grounds.

This home and these parents are an absolute and total answer to prayer for Maria. I know now that God heard and answered our prayers. She has been there more than two years and is getting much better. Time spans between explosions are longer. The parents take these outbursts in their stride and handle each one as they come. The other children are not intimidated by Maria.

I never cease to marvel at God's "coincidences." Maria's foster mother and I have been the best of friends for over ten years. We pray for each other daily, and our families get together often.

It means a lot to me to know that a close friend is able to raise the daughter I couldn't. The beautiful orphan girl from South America has two families—one that loves her and with whom she lives, and one that loves her but cannot bring out the best in her.

THIRTEEN
Street Boy from Calcutta

One day a letter arrived from our nurse friend Cherie Clark in India. She was the one who had rescued Jeremy and his brothers in Vietnam and then later had traveled to Calcutta with her eight children. We owed her a great debt of gratitude. I read the letter over and over with my heart beating wildly. *Why now?* I thought. *Why at this time?*

The letter began:

Aaron is an orphan and a street boy. He was hit by a bus and has a long scar on his arm where he was injured. He was in a hospital, but after his arm healed there was no one to come and claim him and no place for him to go. He was too weak to go out on the streets and beg for his food.

The doctors and nurses didn't know what to do with this little scrap of human-

> *ity until someone thought of contacting me. I went immediately and took Aaron into our children's center and nursed him back to health. Now he needs a permanent home with a mother and a father to cherish and help him. . . .*

The last line said it would cost $3,000—exactly the amount I had saved for a new kitchen—to get this little boy from India to our house.

I looked at the enclosed picture of a handsome, adorable dark-skinned boy with a beaming smile. Across the white border at the bottom of the picture Cherie had written: "Do you think this could possibly be another Scott?"

Of course, I thought, *he looks exactly the way a new Scott family member should look.*

Shortly after we had made our decision to have Aaron come to live with us, our family went to a beautiful Christian retreat center in the mountains, near Silver Creek Falls. There were other children for our young people to swim, hike, and play games with. The adults enjoyed the fellowship, food, singing, good speakers, painting classes, writers' workshops, and plain relaxation.

One morning after breakfast Phil and I sat on the patio, our chairs pulled close together. I rested my head on Phil's shoulder, and we began to pray for our family. A moment later, I jumped up from my chair. "Oh, Phil! Something special has happened. God has given us a promise." I repeated the wondrous words God had put in my mind: "You shall have your little boy *and* your new kitchen." Tears of gratitude and relief ran down my cheeks.

We had reason to cling tightly to that promise in the months to come because it looked as if it would be impossible to have either one. The kitchen money had been spent to bring Aaron, and there was an obstacle to getting Aaron that could be solved only by an act of Congress.

An immigration law stated that each American family could have visas to bring not more than two foreign-born children into the United States for the purpose of adoption.

Getting Marci and Cammi had used up our quota. We couldn't bring any more children.

A bill had been introduced to take the limitation off, but it didn't look as if it would pass. Changes in adoption policies sometimes seem less urgent to people in Congress, I mused. Still, we wrote a lot of letters to chief legislative people, requesting support of this bill. Friends wrote letters, too.

Time went by and the legistlature was nearly ready to recess. We held our breath and prayed. Congress had two calendars: the first was filled with bills that were urgent; the second had inconsequential items and minor issues. On the very last day, all the bills on the second calendar were passed unanimously. When our bill went to the

Senate, they must have seen that it had been passed unanimously—which made it look really good to them.

We felt that God had moved, causing the passage of that bill. Aaron had wanted a home so badly that if the bill hadn't passed, we were convinced that a little brown boy would have been trying to swim clear across the Atlantic Ocean! Still, time moved slowly for all of us, and we spent a long, sometimes frustrating, nine months, waiting for a little boy in India who needed us.

We were grateful that Aaron was living with Cherie and being cared for by her. During our period of waiting for his arrival, we attended a prayer meeting. It was at that time that the Lord beautifully confirmed that Aaron had been chosen for us by the Lord. The Lord also impressed upon us the fact that Aaron was living in a land of darkness, but that he would come to us unmarked and unspoiled. He would be like a pure white flower coming from an inkwell, and his life would show others the glory of the Lord!

We sent gifts to nine-year-old Aaron by way of friends who were traveling to India. Cherie made a calendar for him so he could cross off the days until it was time for him to come. On the front was an airplane with a sign on it that read: TO AMERICA.

We put together a book for Aaron with pictures of all of us. When he went before a judge in India to receive official permission to leave and be adopted, he stepped forward and proudly showed the judge our pictures!

At last everything was arranged on both sides of the mighty ocean. Aaron was due to arrive five days before Christmas.

A friend of ours had a free pass to fly because her husband worked for one of the airlines. She volunteered to fly to New York and escort Aaron to Oregon for us. Her generosity saved us a lot of travel expenses.

It was a cold, clear, star-studded night when our whole family and some of our friends went to the airport to welcome Aaron. I shivered with anticipation, waiting excitedly like a kid at Christmas. *What will he be like? Oh, will he ever come! Maybe he's missed connections along the way.* Just when I thought I couldn't stand it another moment, his plane rolled up to the gate.

When he got off the airplane, he looked so cute, his eyes deep and dark; his hair thick, shiny, and black; his skin brown. Cherie had sent him neatly dressed in black pants, a white cotton shirt, and a bright blue sweater. He looked like a typical handsome little boy from India.

He recognized us instantly from our pictures and came running like a little puppy dog to hug me. He had affectionate hugs for each of us, but he didn't want me out of his sight.

Aaron was from Bengal and spoke the Bengali language. He knew very little English. To compound the problem of communication, Aaron had been born with a speech impediment. *Oh, Lord,* I thought, *isn't a difference in language enough?*

Our new little boy was dear and loving. He would hang on to me, and cry when I was away from him. At first this seemed sweet, but we soon realized we had a very serious problem. Young Aaron had seen so much death (and dying) on the streets of Calcutta, that he had developed an abnormal fear that he and all of us would die. His greatest terror was that I, his new mama, would die.

Every night he woke up crying and shrieking, "Mama die! Mama die!" The whole household would be wakened by his sobs and shouts of fear.

In the daytime it was hard for me to move around the house with him clinging to me. Though I loved him dearly, I began to feel smothered and impatient.

He could hardly bear to have me leave in the mornings. When I would arrive home from work, he would be standing either in the middle of the driveway or beside our country road, waiting for me. On the way home I'd be hoping he wouldn't be so desperate to greet me. As soon as I'd step from the car, though, he would grab me and hug and kiss me over and over again.

The kids began complaining about this small boy who woke them every night with his screams. Phil and I tried to think of ways we could teach Aaron to feel more secure.

Part of the healing began with a game that

Aaron himself made up. Aaron would lie on the floor and tell us he was dead. We had to walk around and around him and pretend we were crying. Suddenly Aaron would jump up and be alive again. He did that over and over until he worked out his fear of death.

Eventually the time came when I had to go to Washington, D.C., for a week to speak at an adoption conference. Aaron had a dreadful time dealing with that. He worried continually: "What if you get lost, Mama? What if I never see you again? Please don't go." My heart wept for him as I tried to reassure him. He would look at me with those deep, dark eyes and then hang his head low. He didn't want me to see his tears.

Jeremy and his brothers, Jeff and Jason, had gone on a camping trip that weekend. Two hours before I had to leave, they returned. Seeing that they had not died, but had actually come back, helped Aaron handle my leaving.

Another time I was going to be away on a business trip for several days. Aaron was so upset that he decided to return to India. He packed his belongings in a little bag and went out to the road in front of our house. He walked up and down, back and forth. Every time he went by, he would peek into the window.

Finally we couldn't stand it any longer. We all ran out and shouted, "Welcome back, Aaron! Glad you are home. Did you have a nice trip?" He laughed and came into the house. It helped him realize that people do "come back."

Gradually Aaron became more secure with us—and less clinging and possessive. I was relieved for myself and happy to see Aaron adjusting better. However, problems with Aaron were more than what first met the eye.

We did not know before Aaron came that he was slightly retarded. We could tell right away that he didn't have a normal ten-year-old's development. Since there was no way to tell his exact age, we figured he was closer to eight years old. His speech impediment made it difficult to understand him.

Special tests revealed that his developmental level ranged between four and one-half and five and one-half years of age. Although we suspected something was wrong, we hadn't been prepared for the truth. It was very hard news to bear. I would look at him and think, *He is so handsome and sweet. Why this extra disadvantage?* It didn't seem fair.

Eventually in school, Aaron began attending a special resource center. The program mainstreams him into some regular classes. He is a delight to his teachers except for his being a little too affectionate, but he is getting that under control. He works without distraction in school, is understanding better, and studies very hard. He learns at a slow but steady pace.

He tries so hard to please. He has decided

to be our sweeper, taking the broom and cleaning every inch of the vinyl floors every day without missing a spot!

One weekend we had an important overnight visitor, General Gosh [pronounced *Goash*], the inspector of prisons in India. PLAN adoption agency had placed some children from Mother Teresa's orphanages and many children Cherie Clark had found and nursed back to health. The general had come to the United States to personally inspect the children who had been adopted from India. His face registered surprise when he saw our international family of legally adopted children.

It was a marvelous experience for Aaron to have someone from India come to see him. He felt so happy and honored to help us welcome our visitor.

Another big surprise was to have Cherie Clark come to our home. Aaron was ecstatic to see her again.

He still remembers her with love, as he often hands me papers from school and pictures he has made, saying, "Here, Mama, send these to Cherie Clark. She would like to have them!"

A few months ago, Aaron hadn't been feeling well for about a day and a half. He complained about a stomachache, but he didn't appear to be very ill, so we weren't overly worried. On that Sunday night, however, he woke at 4:00 A.M. in great pain. Phil rushed him to the emergency room at the hospital, and they decided to admit him for observation. I went to the hospital at eight o'clock and stayed with him all day.

As the hours went by, Aaron's condition seemed to grow more critical. I kept asking the nurse if Aaron was sedated, because I couldn't get a response from him and his skin was cold and clammy. Late in the afternoon the doctor came in and checked Aaron carefully, but he couldn't diagnose the illness.

Suddenly Aaron began to fail rapidly. It seemed to me that he was dying. My first thought was *Aaron is going to love being in Heaven with Jesus. It's going to be so wonderful for him.* My second reaction was *Oh, we are going to miss him. What will we do without our Aaron?* I thought of the verse in the Bible that reassures us that we sorrow not as those who have no hope. I could lose my son through death and still know where he would be.

Doctors and nurses came running and began working over him. Our doctor said he could not stabilize Aaron's condition. Their only hope was to do exploratory surgery. Our pastor and friends came to be with us during the time Aaron was in the operating room.

At one point it appeared that Aaron had died for there was no pulse. Although I felt deep peace, I still felt that the Lord had more in store for Aaron and that it wasn't the right time for him to go.

Miraculously, he rallied. The surgeon told us later that Aaron's appendix had ruptured, spreading poison into his abdominal cavity. He was put into intensive care and connected to life-sustaining equipment. Although the doctors held out no hope for Aaron's survival, we continued to feel God's peace.

We literally lived at the hospital the next eighteen days. For the first few days, Aaron didn't respond at all except to our hugs and kisses, but then he slowly began to show improvement.

I bought him a stuffed elephant, because he had been familiar with elephants in India. One of the nurses put a bandage around the elephant's stomach.

When Aaron was a tiny boy in India, and had been hit by a bus, a policeman had carried him to the hospital. Now he wondered why he didn't have a policeman visiting him during this hospitalization. I wondered how I could work this out! One night as I was walking down the hallway I saw a policeman standing at the reception desk. I introduced myself and told him about Aaron.

The young policeman, whose name was Rick, said that of course he would visit Aaron. The next day he came with bright balloons, a coloring book, and crayons. After that he was a daily visitor. Later he sent me a note thanking me for the opportunity to bring love and comfort to Aaron. He said that in his work he was seldom able to do that.

Soon after Aaron was home and recovering, I met one of his nurses, Kathy, on the street.

She had been the supervisor in intensive care during Aaron's terrible illness.

After she had inquired about Aaron's progress, she said, "Ann, I want you to know what a teaching opportunity it was for me to be able to show the hospital staff how precious and valid are the lives of those who are a little slow—those we label retarded. We were able to observe the way you and Phil and all of his sisters and brothers not only helped him, but cherished him. You spent time with him, showing him how precious he is to you. Aaron was so wonderful and so dear during the whole process.

"Almost everyone in the hospital has experienced a change of attitude toward retarded people. Our staff will never be the same since Aaron's visit!"

Any radio or television program about India catches Aaron's attention immediately. He loves to hear about his native land and listens with interest.

Every day when I come home from work, I see the curtain on the patio door moving. When I open the door, Aaron leaps out from behind the piano and "scares" me. Then he yells, "I love you, Mom."

What a wonderful and loyal little boy! Phil and I adore him. We are grateful that he is here so we can give him the advantages that he needs. When I consider what his life might have been like on the streets of Calcutta if God hadn't rescued him and brought him to us, I can only smile and thank God for his mercy. We look forward to the years ahead and wonder what God has in store for our Aaron from India.

FOURTEEN
A Dangerous Voyage

"In three weeks, two boys will be arriving from a refugee camp in Singapore. Would you like to sponsor them after they come to the United States?"

Would we! That call from the local Lutheran Refugee Service was an answer to prayer. Finally the months and months of phone calls, prayer, and emotional and spiritual pain would have a happy ending.

My thoughts rushed back to that recent period of several years. It began when the Lord had given me an especially heavy sense of the anguish the Southeast Asian refugees were experiencing.

The Lord had put into my mind this thought: *Ann, you can be a link in a chain helping these people. I have two boys in the refugee camps who will be part of your family. In preparation for this, I am going to allow you to experience a little of the brokenheartedness I feel.*

With that, it seemed as if I were connected to the very heart of God. I began to experience almost unbearable pain. From that moment on, I became continually aware of the suffering felt by the refugees.

Phil was the only one who shared even a little of my anguish. He brought me a bouquet of red roses one day after work. "Honey," he began, "I realize a portion of what you are going through. All afternoon there has been a heavy weight around my heart."

It was hard for others to understand why I felt such overwhelming concern for these displaced people, so I stopped trying to explain. In the meantime, I read all I could about their plight—their hopelessness, fear, loss of homes, starvation, separation from families, even death. Thousands had lost their lives at sea. Sometimes when they had tried to land, villagers would wade out and push the frail fishing boats away. They simply had no room or food for a new wave of humanity.

About six months later, after having shared my burden with two dear friends—Virgil, an evangelist, and his precious wife, Roberta—my burden lifted. I would still care and pray for the refugees, but the pain and deep sorrow were gone.

Shortly after that, a Pennsylvania woman who works with refugees contacted me. She told me about two Vietnamese children still in Thailand—two brothers named Vinh and Tran. *Oh, maybe these are the two boys the Lord promised me,* I thought excitedly, little realizing how hard it would be to bring them over here.

At that time, in mid-1978, the United States Refugee Program was not yet in operation. At that point the two brothers had no way of getting to America. Nevertheless, our family eagerly began to make plans for their arrival.

Phil and I were so proud of our sons as each one offered his room, bed, or clothing. Each understood something of what it meant to live in a refugee camp. We corresponded with Vinh and Tran, who by that time had become Christians. We learned more about their terrifying boat trip to freedom, and then of the squalid conditions in the Singapore camp.

I became more emotionally involved as each letter came and I was more persistent in writing to government officials for their help in getting the boys out of the camp and into our home. My letters were to no avail. No avenue was open then for unaccompanied minor children to come to the United States.

One of my contacts advised me to get in touch with a Lutheran refugee service in Pennsylvania. I phoned across the United States and spoke to a Vietnamese man about my problem and related information about the boys. Finally I gave him the boys' names.

There was silence. Then with a loud shout,

he exclaimed, "Those are my nephews! I didn't know where they were. We have been searching, hoping to hear from them, praying they were still alive!" The overjoyed man tried to get his nephews into the United States, but he encountered as many blind alleys as I had. In the process, though, he discovered another uncle living in France. There was success this time, for France opened its doors and received the boys.

We were grateful the boys were now safe, but felt sad that they weren't coming to live with us. Already a year and a half had gone by since God's promise of two boys from the refugee camps. *Have we somehow missed the ones God intended for us?* I wondered.

Suddenly I recalled something else God had impressed upon me: *You can be used as a link in a chain helping these people.* That was it. I had been able to help unite Vinh and Tran with their uncle in France. Nothing had been wasted.

A few months later, my interest in refugee children was still fresh. By that time, the United States government had given permission to sponsor minor children and bring them to this country. What joy and relief I and other concerned people experienced at the news. Soon after, we were notified that two boys were in a refugee camp and needed sponsors. They were Le Van Tien and Naow. Tien was sixteen, Naow was fifteen, and both boys were Buddhists.

"Oh, Phil," I stammered. "Will it be wise to have these boys in our home?" We thought of Vinh and Tran who were solid Christians and would have fit into our family perfectly.

Phil replied thoughtfully, "Tien and Naow need the same opportunity to find Christ as anyone else. Let's take the chance and invite them."

A few evenings later the case worker brought Tien and Naow to our home. They were handsome boys. Neither one spoke English. Our son Jeremy, who is Vietnamese, immediately stepped forward, shook hands, and then embraced them. He made introductions and was able to translate for all of us. Later Jeremy confided, "Tien and Naow think we live in a mansion and that you and Dad must be extremely wealthy."

The boys followed Jeremy around in the days that followed, and Jeremy began to teach them English. A bond of love grew among the three of them. After a few weeks, Tien and Naow asked for American names. "This is our new life now. We want to be like Americans," they explained via our interpreter son Jeremy.

At first we all made suggestions, but Phil had the best idea: "Jeremy, you choose their names."

We were glad when he chose names from the Bible, James and John. Tien's new name was John, and Naow became James. From the beginning it became obvious that James is a happy-go-lucky, fun-loving, boisterous, and impetuous young man, while John is sentimental, loving, and musically gifted. Both are excellent soccer players. After James and John joined, we had five boys from our family on the school and city soccer teams. Our whole family turned out often to cheer them on to victory and to sympathize after a few defeats!

The boys began learning English quickly. We wanted them to attend the best school we could find. St. James, a private Catholic school in McMinnville, seemed to be it. The nuns there treated them as individuals, loving and encouraging them along their way.

With Jeremy's help, James and John told us about their escape and rescue. They had been boyhood friends living in a small village and working together on fishing boats. When the Viet Cong took over Vietnam, James and John were "old enough" to be drafted into the communist army. Many parents would send their teen-aged boys away rather than have them serve under the harsh Viet Cong rule.

One day when James and John were fishing, they saw a boat with thirty-two refugees on board. They had not planned to escape, but they both realized this was their chance. Within minutes they made a decision that was to completely change their lives. They jumped overboard and swam to the refugee boat. On the open sea they were subject to the elements. They would not have survived if other passengers had not shared precious food and water.

After ten days at sea they saw an American Navy transport ship operating with the Seventh Fleet. Their little boat had developed several leaks, so when the large ship came alongside and rescue operations began, they cried and cheered.

Just after all thirty-four refugees were on board, they looked back at their tiny vessel bobbing in the huge ocean. It made a last dip and sank beneath the swells. Help had come just in time or they all would have drowned.

Richard Smith, one of the divers on the ship, befriended the two half-starved boys, fed and clothed them, and applied medicine to their sores. He later showed them around the ship when they were stronger. (To this day the boys keep in touch with Richard, writing to him often.) The ship took the survivors to a refugee camp in Singapore.

How grateful we were to the Lord for protecting our two boys. Shortly after they came to live with us, we discovered that John had a heart murmur. One day Phil and I took him to a doctor in Portland for a long series of tests. By the end of the day, we all felt exhausted.

As we pulled into the driveway, the kids ran out to the car to greet us. "Happy Anniversary, Mom and Dad! We pooled our money and want you two to go to a nice restaurant and have dinner." In the rush of the day and our concern for John, I'd forgotten all about our anniversary. I groaned inwardly, thinking I would fall asleep in my soup. The kids were insistent. Phil and I drove to the nearest restaurant and ate a fine dinner. We also enjoyed a rare quiet time together to talk.

"Phil," I reminisced, "did you ever dream we would have all these children?"

Phil laughed. "One thing is certain, Ann. We never have a dull moment. We're lucky to have a quiet one!"

Revived and in much better spirits, we drove back home. "Oh, no!" Phil exclaimed as we turned into the driveway. "The lights are out!" We hurried to the door to see what new calamity had befallen us.

"Surprise, surprise!" The lights blazed on, revealing giggling children and many of our dearest friends. The house was decorated with fresh flowers, candles, red hearts, and signs proclaiming, "We love you, Mom and Dad." Phil and I grabbed each child for a quick hug.

Favorite snacks, a lovely pink and white decorated cake, and pink punch crowded our big oval table. For entertainment, the kids had organized a highly original band. The steady drumbeat of chopsticks tapping on an empty Coke bottle or on an upside-down metal bowl accompanied Cammi on the piano, Susan playing the flute, and the sweet sounds of Marci's clarinet. Special lighting effects came from a slotted spoon over a high intensity lamp.

One of the highlights of the evening was when James and John serenaded us with tender love songs sung in Vietnamese, using make-believe microphones. One delightful surprise after another was provided by our inventive children. Never before had there been an anniversary of our marriage to equal this one!

Not long after this, Virgil, our evangelist friend, began to take a special interest in James and John. He was also a fisherman and owned a fishing boat, so he and the boys shared a common interest in fishing. Virgil often came to our house, carrying a big ice chest filled with a day's fresh catch. Virgil, James, and John worked together, cleaning and cutting up the fish. Then the boys cooked them Vietnamese-style. What an incomparable feast they prepared for us.

As I mentioned earlier, James and John were Buddhists when they came to us. They wanted to fit into our family and be like us, and especially like Jeremy. Although we did not press them to become Christians, James and John willingly, almost eagerly, went to church with us every Sunday. There doesn't seem to be any one thing that brought the boys to accept Jesus as their Savior. Instead it was a combination of Virgil's friendship, the loving acceptance from their new family, the care and concern from the sisters at the

Catholic school, and a movie they saw about Jesus.

On the screen they watched miracles, and were impressed when Jesus touched people who had leprosy. At his touch the dead white flesh became alive again. The boys' hearts opened, and they came to know and accept this Jesus who loves and heals.

Eventually, we located their parents. The boys send money, supplies, and long letters to them. Each day Phil and I pray with James and John for their families in Vietnam.

Sometimes when I am tired, I remember how God spoke to a bone-weary woman. I am eternally grateful for these two sons.

FIFTEEN
An Enchanted Evening

One spring evening in 1981 Phil was helping the children with their homework. The weather had turned warm, and the sweet scent of lilacs and daphne drifted through the open windows. I looked up from mending one of Mark's shirts. An overwhelming feeling of gratitude flooded my heart as I gazed around the room. *What a marvelous family God has given us!* I thought.

As I went back to my sewing, I began to wonder if the children knew how much Phil and I loved them. Oh, we told them often, but perhaps they didn't realize how special they were as individuals.

There must be a way we can give them a tangible expression of our love that they will always remember. But what could we do? I knew it would not be easy in a family as large and varied as ours.

During the next few days a plan began to form in my mind. At the dinner table several nights later, I asked everyone a question: "What do you think about having a Family Night Awards Banquet?"

Lisa and Christina, with their usual exuberance, yelled, "Oh, boy, let's have one!"

"How would we do that, Mom?" always practical April asked. Frankly I wasn't quite sure myself.

Jeremy smiled. "I would be glad to help."

Enthusiasm spread as the idea caught fire. Phil and I divided the family into committees with something for everyone. There were menu-planning, cooking, decorating, table setting, entertainment committees, and even a cleanup detail. During the following week, what had been a sketchy plan began to take shape.

Through the following month the house buzzed with conspiratorial whispers and shouts of excitement as the children developed their plans and carried them out. Papers, paste, scissors, and marking pens filled a corner of the playroom. Some committees kept their ideas secret until time for the banquet.

I was the sole member of the Awards Presentation Committee! It took me nearly a week to write an individual message for each child. I complimented their positive characteristics such as being kind, dependable, honest, or generous. (Some, I admit, were hoped-for attributes!) Each message ended with words of appreciation for that child's willingness to share his or her love and "Christlike spirit" with the family.

A close friend wrote the words in calligraphy, and a printer made professional copies on fine parchment paper. I was impressed by the way they looked, so I went a step further and had each printed copy mounted on wood and made into a plaque.

As I held one of the plaques in my hand, I began to pray, "Oh, Lord, help me be a real encouragement to our children. Let them know how loved and special they are. I thank you for each one of them."

When the long-awaited awards evening arrived, we were more than ready for the festivities to begin. This was a special event to the last detail. Colored streamers waved from every room. An enticing, spicy fragrance of food filled the air. Signs posted by the decorating committee proclaimed such messages as "First Annual Awards Dinner," "Hurray for the Scotts," and a modest, "We're No. 1."

Each family member was scrubbed and wearing Sunday-best clothes. The girls had taken great care in fixing their hair.

We had deciced to make the dinner a formal affair. The table looked as though it were ready for a display in the finest china shop window. Our best blue and white dishes were set on a white lace tablecloth. In the center of the table was an exquisite arrangement of pink and red roses, baby's breath, and white daisies set in a crystal bowl. Pink candles burned with a soft glow.

Before we ate, we joined hands, and each of us in turn thanked the Lord for something about our family.

Jeremy's brother Jason had prepared a Vietnamese banquet for us. We feasted on delicate egg flower soup, lettuce salad, Vietnamese-style chicken, marinated beef, fried rice, and bamboo shoots.

After dinner the entertainment committee presented skits. Then we played hilarious parodies of television shows, such as "Make Me Laugh" and "This Is Your Life." We laughed until we nearly fell out of our chairs.

My heart was pounding when it was my turn to present the awards. The kids bounced into the living room and relaxed on the soft yellow couches that form a semicircle for easy conversation. I stood up to tell the children how grateful to God we were for each one of them. I held back tears as I told them how much we loved them and how proud we were of them and their achievements.

Phil stepped forward and put his arms around me. Without his love and support, without his tender heart and compassion for needy children, I knew we would not have had this wonderful family. Together Phil and I presented a plaque and a few words to each child. As each youngster stepped forward, he or she received an enthusiastic round of applause and whistles from the other children.

Their hugs, proud smiles, and shining faces were a great reward. Our celebration, with all its events, turned out to be even more fulfilling than I had imagined.

The menu-planning committee had one last surprise. When we walked into the kitchen, there were huge containers of vanilla and chocolate ice cream. We were invited to make our own sundaes from a tempting array of fresh fruits, syrups, hot fudge, nuts, coconut, and clouds of whipping cream.

We had a grand evening and learned to feel very good about ourselves at the First Annual Scott Family Awards Banquet!

PART TWO
Other Challenges

SIXTEEN
*House
of the
Open Door*

Through the years people have often asked
me, "Where do you put that many children?"
and "How in the world do you feed and
clothe them all?" Questions like these arise
from natural curiosity, considering the prices
of things these days. The most obvious
aspect of living at the Scotts involves our
housing arrangement. When Phil and I were
first married, we built a small one-bedroom
house. Gradually as our family grew, we
added to the existing structure. Our first addition consisted of four new bedrooms and
two baths.

After six months, we again took up hammers and nails and said good-bye to any
semblance of social life. This time we added a
family room with a large fireplace, a double
garage, a laundry room, another bedroom,
and a big pantry for storing fruits and

vegetables. In 1975 when we adopted Mark—our thirteenth member of the family—we ran out of dining-room table space. We prayed for a new table for several months, thanking the Lord in advance for his provision.

One day our neighbors Ted and Harriet Gahr brought over a young Chinese man named Hong, his wife, and two small boys. They had recently escaped from Communist Vietnam. Hong needed a job and did not want to go on welfare to support his family. As I looked at Hong, the word *table* came into my mind and stayed there. By using a lot of hand motions, I was able to communicate that we would like him to build a table for us. Hong smiled and nodded and then left with his family and the neighbors.

The next day we returned the visit. I was thrilled when I saw that Hong had drawn a perfect plan for a table. Picturing our entire family sitting around the table with plenty of elbow room filled me with anticipation. We soon learned that Hong had been a woodworking craftsman in Vietnam.

The large oval table he made for us turned out to be gorgeous and filled our needs perfectly. Here was another instance of God's providing in a special way for our family.

Next we needed more bedrooms for our six girls. When the table was finished, we asked Hong if he would be willing to build new bedrooms for us. All our negotiations were in sign language. He nodded and smiled.

We had no money to pay Hong, but we felt that the Lord was asking us to employ him, partly so that he could learn the English language and American customs and then be employable in the job market, and partly so that we could have our bedrooms. All that long cold winter, he built for us. The amazing thing was that every two weeks, we could pay Hong. The money always came in. By spring we had our lovely bedroom-bath addition consisting of six bedrooms built around a central playroom and bathroom. A deck winds all the way around the outside. Each girl has her room decorated to suit her individual taste.

After that, we asked Hong to build a large covered front deck, so the kids would have a place to play in any kind of weather. He wanted to know the style. I knew he was tired of our western style, so I told him, "Chinese." Hong really came to life.

With great enthusiasm he curved the rafters on the ends and put lattice work on the sides. We decorated it like an indoor garden and filled it with pots of blooming geraniums and petunias. I know Hong was disappointed when we stained it to match the house. He would have preferred it lacquered a brilliant red.

By the time Hong was finished, all the materials and labor were completely paid for. He was able to support his wife and two children, and also learned American customs from people who understood and appreciated his culture.

A little later in the year Phil and I felt the need to have a place in our home where we could sit and talk together in private. We hit upon the idea of converting our double garage into a bedroom-bath-sitting area for *two*. My desk would be in there along with my typewriter. We decorated the area in red and white and made it quite comfortable—in fact, too comfortable. Instead of affording us privacy, it has become the most popular area in the house.

After our house was remodeled, I became even more aware of an ugly problem: our back yard. It was an eyesore. One warm spring day I stood on the back deck and surveyed the ruins. Then I thought of the verse, "You have not because you ask not." I began to pray aloud softly, "Lord, I want to ask if there is some way the yard could be landscaped as a special favor for me?"

A few weeks later I went to a nearby college to hear a presentation of C. S. Lewis's works. Afterward, as I was about to leave, I glanced around and saw a friend named Donna I hadn't visited with for a number of years. We had been in a prayer group together, and then our paths had gone separate ways. Now chatting again after all that time, we renewed our neglected friendship. I told her about our family and some of the miracles God had performed in our lives.

Toward the end of our conversation, I remembered her artistic talent for designing yards. "Donna, do you still do landscaping?"

"Yes. In fact, I'm a professional landscaper."

I told her about our dreary back yard. She promised to stop by and tell me what could be done.

True to her promise, she came to our house the very next week. I loved her ideas for our yard *and* our family. "Ann, I think with a little direction, your children could do the work!" she exclaimed.

The next Saturday Donna was at our door with fifty pounds of grass seed, fertilizer, and a truckload of trees and plants. Faithfully, she came every Saturday. She was like a cheerleader: "Joe, you dig the holes here in the shade for the rhododendron bushes. Phil, dig over there for the roses. Be careful! Paul, this is the way you prepare the ground for grass seed. Don't forget to keep it wet after you plant it."

Gradually the back yard began looking better and better. We had a time keeping the younger kids and dogs out of the yard while everything was growing, but finally the tiny shoots of grass became a thick, luxuriant, weed-free emerald carpet. Shrubs and trees made a border, and the flower beds were a riot of color that lasted all summer long.

In September I telephoned her. "Donna, the yard is lovelier than I dreamed it would be. We are delighted. Please send your bill."

"Ann, I didn't mention it to you, but I felt very low when I ran into you that evening at college. When you told me about your family and how real God is to you and the miracles he is doing in your life, I remembered what it was like to feel close to him. I have looked forward to coming to your house each week, and my faith has grown stronger. I have you to thank for that. The new yard is my gift to you."

My faith was strengthened, too, when I saw how God had answered my prayer.

Even after the landscaping and the remodeling of our house were finished, we still had a very small kitchen. In fact, it was much smaller than most kitchens. Here we were, with all those hungry children—and only one burner of the stove worked. I think you could say it worked; it had two speeds— high or off! The oven didn't cooperate at all. We cooked mountains of food in two large electric frying pans for a year.

The refrigerator was another challenge. Where could we store the twenty dozen eggs, five gallons of milk, and huge boxes of fresh vegetables and fruit we consumed each week? A typical weekend snack for us consisted of at least a case of oranges and a bushel of apples.

One day I grew tired of it all. I had burned breakfast, and a dozen eggs had fallen from a balancing act on the refrigerator shelves into a scrambled frenzy on the floor. After a few tears of frustration, I walked over to my little kitchen window, looked across the green meadow and declared in a loud voice. "Praise the Lord for my new kitchen!"

A nearby youngster looked at me suspiciously with narrowed eyes. "What new kitchen?"

I pointed out the window. "It's right out there. Can't you see it? Why, it's big enough to roller-skate in!"

"Oh, Mom!"

Every single day I praised the Lord aloud for my new kitchen, even though I didn't know how I would get it. We began saving. It didn't seem as if we could ever have enough, but I put every spare penny, nickel, and dime into our kitchen account. I danced through the house with sheer joy the day our passbook showed $3,000, the amount we needed for the foundation. We could start on our new kitchen immediately. To celebrate, we took all the children to McDonald's for hamburgers.

Before that week went by, we had an urgent request from our nurse friend, Cherie Clark. She asked us to take a boy from India into our home. How does one choose between a kitchen and a little boy with huge brown eyes and no home?

Phil and I talked it over, and it seemed to us that there was no choice. We might be this boy's only chance to have a home and parents.

I withdrew our savings, and we started the process of bringing ten-year-old Aaron to

America. That sent us right back to square one. We were batting 1.000 as far as kids were concerned, but 000 toward our kitchen! Nevertheless, I couldn't give up.

A long, cold winter stretched before us. Even though we had no money, I wanted to do something positive about our new kitchen.

I began to haunt the library, checking out every book I could find about kitchens. All that winter, we collected ideas. We laughed over silly suggestions. No, each child couldn't have his own little refrigerator. No, we couldn't have a robot to serve the meals and wash dishes.

After months of filling wastepaper baskets, we had our plans, perfect in every way except one. We had no money with which to implement them. When a warm and welcome spring ushered winter out that year, something unexpected happened. We had a marvelous gift, $5,000 from the sale of property Phil's dad had owned. What a joyful spring that was! We began work on the kitchen immediately, not knowing the financial straits we would soon be in.

We had the foundation built and the framing done when Phil called me at my office one day. I could tell immediately that something was wrong. "Ann, the mill has closed. After working for thirty years in the plywood business, I lost my job today."

It took me a minute to grasp what he was saying.

"Oh, Phil, I'm sorry. Don't worry. We'll be all right."

Even while I was trying to say the right words to comfort Phil, I wondered how we could possibly manage when we had so many expenses.

We had to let the carpenter go, and Phil took over the work. It was a frustrating time. When the budget didn't stretch far enough for food and building supplies, he had to stop building. We lived on my salary from the adoption center and his unemployment insurance. After a few months Phil found another job, but it took a whole year to buy the appliances and finish our kitchen.

As we look back, we realize that God meant for us to have that winter to draw plan after plan. It gave us the chance to design an efficient and beautiful kitchen that is exactly right for our large family.

There is a breakfast-and-lunch preparation center. At one time, sixteen school and work lunches were prepared and packed there, five days a week. A built-in toaster and microwave oven slide neatly into a cupboard and out of sight when not in use.

The dish and silverware cupboards and drawers open from both the kitchen and dining room sides for easy table-setting. There is a bake center that has fifty-pound bins for flour, sugar, rice, and so on. Folding cupboard doors close off the mixer, blender, and spices. We have lots of counter space.

We also have locked cabinets for chocolate chips, coconut, potato chips, and other tempting snack items that would quickly disappear if not protected.

One of the best additions is our walk-in refrigerator, which is about the size of a small bedroom. The refrigerator unit was no more expensive than buying a refrigerator. Phil built it and paneled it in the same wood as the rest of the house. We also have two freezers and three meat lockers!

We have tried to bring the feeling of the outdoors into the house. The walls are natural barn cedar. The counter tops are cream-colored tile. The vinyl floor covering for the kitchen and dining room looks as if it has pebbles in it.

We have windows all the way across two sides of the kitchen. Through one we can see the spectacular view of the trees on the gently rolling hills behind our house. The other windows let me watch the kids when they are swimming in our large above-ground pool. Sliding glass doors connect the dining room to a wooden sun deck leading to the back yard or swimming pool.

Our kids all enjoy the recreation these areas provide, not to mention the wooded acreage which makes such fine hiking territory. We're very thankful that our home has become a truly spacious and efficient one, helping to meet the many needs of our large family.

SEVENTEEN
"What's for Supper?"

Another topic of perennial interest is food. In a family the size of ours, someone is always eating or cooking. With the varied cultures and eating habits, it's a challenge to have everyone happily fed. I don't know how we could manage if it weren't for the fact that we raise much of our own meat, poultry, fruits, and vegetables.

We keep twenty head of cattle and raise the hay to feed them. The kids take turns milking Daisy, Petunia, and Blossom—the three milk cows. We get ham, sausage, and fresh pork from the pigs we keep, and chickens provide a plentiful supply of wholesome eggs.

Our huge garden provides us with bushels of tasty fruits and vegetables. Phil prepares the ground, and everyone plants the seeds the day before Memorial Day. After that, we take turns watering and weeding.

All summer long we're richly rewarded with fresh fruits and vegetables. Whatever we don't consume right away, we freeze or can. We freeze strawberries, little June peas, corn, and spinach. Winter squash and potatoes keep well all winter.

The girls and I usually can around two thousand quarts of fruits and vegetables during the summer. We make an assembly line to prepare and can vegetables and fruits from our trees—cherries, nectarines, peaches, pears, and plums. What a colorful scene our storeroom shelves make when they're filled—like something from a county fair minus the blue ribbons!

Besides the beef, pork, poultry, and dairy products, rice is a main staple of our diet. I've learned to cook it many ways. Soy sauce is poured over Korean fried rice, while Vietnamese fried rice is cooked with a fish sauce available in the Oriental section of some grocery stores.

We also eat lots of fresh vegetables and fruits, tossed green salads, stir-fried vegetables, egg rolls, egg dishes (scrambled or in noodles), fried rice, and homemade granola.

Strangely enough, I've discovered one food every child likes, no matter where they are from—spaghetti! Our favorite dessert is ice-cream sundae or pie.

Most of our girls like to bake, so we have lots of homemade treats—cinnamon rolls,

chocolate or oatmeal cookies, and brownies.
All winter long the tantalizing aroma of
freshly baked bread fills the house.

Quite often we invite other large families to
come home from church with us for turkey or
roast beef and all the trimmings from our
storehouse of carefully preserved foods.

Earlier, I mentioned the monks at the
Trappist abbey. One day I received a surprise
phone call from Father Paschal, their
business manager. "Mrs. Scott, we are able
to buy damaged restaurant supply goods
from the ship docks. Usually there are more
supplies than we can use. We would like to
share some with your family."

It is the highlight of the month when
Father Paschal turns into our driveway.
Shouts of "He's here! He's here!" echo
through the house and bounce off the walls.
The children race out to meet him. He smiles
and throws open the van doors.

Suddenly it's like Christmas. Excitement
fairly crackles through the air because we
never know what will be in the big boxes.
The kids open them and yell, "Look at this!
See what's in this one!" There is usually
enough rice (we use 100 pounds of rice a
month), flour, and sugar to keep us supplied
until Father Paschal comes again. Sometimes
there are pudding or cake mixes. Often there
are mysterious, unlabeled cans of food.

We laughed the time we opened a case of
filled pepper shakers. We have found boxes
of dishes, a thousand paper cups, a fifty-

pound sack of salt, and little individual restaurant-type packages of jam and jelly. One hundred pounds of sesame seeds sent us searching through the recipe books. For a while, we had sesame seeds on everything. The kids' all-time favorite find was seventy-five pounds of after-dinner mints.

A recent surprise was fourteen huge boxes of delicious puff pastry. It turned us into creative bakers. I made fifty-four cream puffs, which I took to a church potluck dinner one Sunday night.

The gourmet items are especially fun. We have eaten eight gallons of pickled artichoke hearts and three cases of water chestnuts. We especially loved the dozen boxes of frozen carrot cakes with cream cheese frosting! Recently we had a candlelight dinner and dined elegantly on smoked quail.

Soon after that first phone call from Father Paschal, the abbey sent us a letter along with a generous check. The words blurred as I read through tear-filled eyes: "We want to reach out and help you because you and your family have shown us the love of Christ in action. We will be sending a check each month for additional groceries."

More important than the money and the food is the knowledge that we are mentioned in their prayers. God not only helps us have a bountiful supply of food, but also cares for us in every way.

We have a firm rule in our house. Everyone in the family must eat the evening meal together and remain at the table at least twenty minutes after the meal to visit. We begin our mealtime by holding hands and singing a blessing. Occasionally we appoint one person to be in charge of the dinner conversation. Sometimes we learn Bible verses together after dinner. We usually work on one chapter for a month with everyone saying it together until we all learn it. We've memorized several psalms that way. Currently we're working on First Corinthians, chapter 13.

As I look around the table and remember each child's past, I marvel at the way God has brought us together. While we simmered and stewed, he stirred us with his love. Patiently, he is blending and shaping us into a family.

EIGHTEEN
Love and Blessings

In this day of tight money, people want to know how we manage. Phil and I have asked each other the same thing many times! After each child comes to live with us, we are content. "We don't have the room or the money for any more children," we say. But when the next needy child comes along and we say, "Yes," God provides for us—sometimes in unusual ways.

One example which continually warms our hearts is of a dear lady who sends us fifteen dollars a month from her small social security check. She says she is too old to take in children herself, and she wants to help. I know the Lord will reward her with an equal share of what we are doing.

As each need is met, it comes as a delightful surprise—and just at the right time. Last fall we faced another of those economic tests of faith. The overwhelming amount of $1,000 was due on our insurance policy. Just about that time Phil and I were on a Christian television program, "The Gary Randall Show." We talked about our family, but we were careful not to mention the financial need we had. As a result of the show, God's goodness prompted a woman we had never met, or even heard of, to mail us a check. I'm sure you can guess the amount: $1,000.

When I opened that envelope and saw that $1,000 check, I screamed excitedly and ran through the house to show Phil and the rest of the family our answer to prayer.

Because we've been so blessed, we've established a household tradition. As soon as we take a youngster into our home, we begin sending money in the child's name to a missionary. The Scriptures tell us, "Give and it shall be given unto you." We believe we have to do our part first.

Just as the people who have helped us share in what we are doing, we believe we have a share in the missionaries' work. The money we send each month is an encouragement to the missionaries. They write to the children and sometimes visit! Our youngsters begin to catch the joy of giving as they see firsthand the results of being generous. We pray this will become a permanent part of their lives.

Jeremy and Joe help support Elmer, a little boy from Guatemala, to whom they write and send money every month. Frequently they get a letter from Elmer. We all share in their excitement as Jeremy or Joe proudly reads the letter to us at the dinner table. Paul sends money to support a tiny girl in Ethiopia.

Late one summer, Phil's dad died. Phil and I immediately became involved in making funeral arrangements, looking after Phil's mother and taking care of the necessary legal matters.

We were caught up in the details until one morning I looked at the calendar. It was nearly time for school to start, and we needed money to buy all the clothes, shoes, and school supplies the children had to have. I knelt beside my bed and began to pray: "Lord, you know your children have needs. Please help us."

God has perfect timing and is never late. Two days later a $500 check came in the mail. The enclosed note said: "Dear Ann, I believe you need this money for your children's school supplies."

Since the donor lived nearby, I personally thanked her and let her know how much the money meant to us. She was thrilled because it was the first time she had felt God urge her to send money to anyone. When I left, she gave me a big hug. She seemed almost as happy in giving the check as we were to receive it!

That afternoon a social worker named Bill came to our adoption office. He had accompanied a child from New York for a local couple to adopt. I felt my spirit drawn to Bill. I sensed a soul who was lost and lonely.

As soon as he left, I began to pray: "Lord, if you will bring him back into my office, I will be bold and talk to him about you. He needs your love and assurance."

Thirty minutes later, I was getting ready to leave for the day when I heard footsteps slowly coming up the stairs. In the doorway stood Bill, smiling timidly. "May I come in?" he asked.

Motioning him to a chair by my desk, I thought, *How tired and unsure he looks.* "How are you, Bill?" I asked. We exchanged pleasantries and discussed the child he had brought and the couple who would be adopting him.

Breathing a quick, silent prayer, I suddenly asked, "Bill, have you ever given any thought to where you will be spending eternity?" His dark eyes opened wide, and he jumped from the shock of my question.

"Mrs. Scott, if I had any evidence that God existed, I would believe."

My first thought was of the check in my purse. I told Bill about my asking God's help for my children and the way God had urged a woman I barely knew to respond. I opened my purse and put the check for $500 in his hand.

Tears welled up in his eyes, and he swallowed hard. After several minutes of silence, he finally spoke, barely above a whisper. "God really does care about us, doesn't he?" he said, looking down at the check. "Do you think he could love me—even after some of the things I've done? I want to believe." He hesitated. "Would you tell me more about him?"

I had the absolute joy of telling Bill about the God who loves and forgives us and who gives us eternal life through his Son, Jesus Christ.

At the end, Bill bowed his head and said simply, "I believe. I believe." When he looked up, his eyes were clear and shining. All fear was gone. In its place was peace.

I praised the Lord for the donor of that $500 check. Not only had it come at a special time of need for our kids, but it had also been a turning point to lead Bill to the Lord. What a wonderful God we have!

NINETEEN
"Two Days Off for Good Behavior"

As important as the physical needs are, Phil and I know that meeting the spiritual and emotional needs of our kids is even more important. Some come to us with deep hurts that require a tremendous amount of healing. Adopted children ask not only, "Who am I?" but "Who am I really?"

One question that often comes up, especially after a speaking engagement, is "How do you discipline all those children?" It isn't easy!

If there is a problem, Phil and I go into our room to cool off and talk it over. We pray together for the offender—and then for the most helpful solution. We pray together until we find God's direction. Usually Phil talks to the child alone. Sometimes only a talk is needed.

We've established certain "house rules"

and expect them to be obeyed. An infraction of the rules might mean washing all the dishes for a week (that's a lot of dishes)—with two days off for good behavior. We find that makes a good incentive!

Sometimes a child has to spend an evening or two in his room thinking of how he might have done better.

A daughter's unloving attitude may mean that she has to learn Bible verses about love. If a son has been irresponsible in school, he has to write an essay on responsibility.

The kids usually wash dishes for three days for "mouthing off." Phil won't allow any disrespect toward me or anyone else.

Because we are a family with such unique challenges, the whole family goes twice a month for counseling. Some of the children still feel anger and pain from their experiences in the past. Some have felt much rejection, hurt, fears, and guilt.

Phil and I occasionally go for counseling alone. As in any family, parents are often the targets when the children hurl darts of anger. We seem like safe targets to them because we love them. Even so, we often feel intense pain and anguish from their frustrated outbursts.

I recall a difficult time when we had one serious crisis after another. Each time something would happen, Phil and I would go into our bedroom, shut the door, and ask the Lord for help. His help was exactly what we needed. However, the rest of our family was sometimes left wondering about our disappearances. In fact, our daughter April became so puzzled that she called our daughter Cindy on the telephone to say, "What do you think is going on here with Mom and Dad? They just keep going into their bedroom and shutting the door!"

TWENTY
Adoption Days

While we have our problems, our family is united by love and many warm traditions. One of the most exciting is Adoption Day.

When some people see Phil and me with all our children, they assume we are foster parents, but Phil and I have adopted each child. Every time an adoption of a child is finalized, we turn that day into an occasion of joyous celebration.

On the day before, each child proudly carries a note from us to his teacher: "Tomorrow is Adoption Day. Our child won't be in school!" Relatives, friends, and other big families with adopted children are invited.

On that very special day we all wear our best clothes. The one being adopted leads the group into the courthouse. On the first few occasions we were able to fit into the judge's office, but now we use the biggest courtroom.

As the kids skip along over the polished floors, there are lots of whispers: "Do you remember the day you were adopted?" "Yeah, do you?"

The judge knows us well by now, and he is almost as happy as we are. Any attempt to be solemn or dignified flies out the window. We take lots of pictures.

After all the papers we filled out to get the child in the first place, the actual adoption ceremony is simple. It takes place after the child has been living with us for about a year. The judge asks if we want to adopt the child. Then he asks the youngster if he would like to be adopted. While the judge signs the adoption decree, the children jump up and there are hugs and kisses and laughter. I usually feel as if a brass band should be playing.

As part of our celebration the whole group goes out to eat together. Usually, we go to a pizza parlor and order the biggest pizzas on the menu, along with pitchers of soft drinks.

After lunch we have "open house." Our home is gaily decorated with colorful balloons and streamers. Friends come by to congratulate us, and we serve homemade cake and ice cream.

Phil and I give a warm letter of welcome and a special gift to our newly adopted child. Some of the girls have enjoyed a commemorative plate with the year painted or engraved on it. Often we give a Bible with an appropriate message and date on the front page.

People have sometimes asked us about our second-birth-daughter, Cindy, wondering if she didn't feel deprived by giving up so much to be part of a super big family. A few incidents come to mind. I will let them speak for themselves.

One day when Cindy was a young teenager, we were standing at the sink doing dishes together. She began telling about the dress one of her classmates had just purchased. She described it in great detail. I sensed the longing in her voice.

"Oh, Cindy," I said, "I wish I could buy you a dress just like that."

Her immediate response was "That's all right, Mom. She probably doesn't have any brothers or sisters."

Another time, when Cindy came home from school, she said, "Mother, people keep asking me how it feels to have so many adopted kids in our family."

I stopped peeling potatoes and asked, "How do you answer that question, Cindy?"

"Well, I never know exactly what to say, so I tell them it feels just fine because they are all my brothers and sisters." Once when Cindy and I were preparing dinner, I asked her how she felt about having to go without so many nice things. "Mom, I have received *more than material things* from my brothers and sisters. I have learned to love handicapped children, retarded children, people from other countries. I have been able to grow up without prejudices. They are my brothers and sisters, and I'm so proud of each one of them. I know I have received the finest gifts of all."

We were elated when Cindy and Tom announced their engagement seven years ago. We have known and loved Tom since he was a blond, blue-eyed little boy we used to pick up on Sunday mornings and take to Sunday school.

Cindy wanted all of her brothers and sisters in her Christmas wedding. She and Tom insisted that Mark be their best man. It didn't bother them that Mark could barely hobble. When the time came, they proudly watched and silently cheered as Mark haltingly made his way up the aisle.

Phil and I thank God for our forever family. He has blessed us and filled our home with love and with the realization that because of him, there is always room for one more.

EPILOGUE
An Update

The years speed by. The house that once echoed the unsteady tapping of toddlers' small feet now reverberates to the fast drumbeat of teen-agers rushing through.

Time has brought about many changes in our children except for thirty-three-year-old *Phyllis*, our first-born. She is still receiving loving care in an institution in Salem. Our whole family visits her often. I believe that someday in heaven she'll know that, in a way, she was responsible for our adopting our lovely big family.

Here is current news about the rest of the family in the order in which you met them in this book:

Cindy, twenty-six, our second-born, was married in December 1977. She and her husband, Tom, have made us grandparents. Charity, five, and Stacey, two, come to visit one night a week. They have a glorious time playing hide-and-seek or horseyback riding on their aunts' and uncles' backs. Charity bangs on my typewriter, puts on my makeup, smiles at me, and says, "I love you, Grandma."

Angie, eighteen, is strikingly blonde among her dark-haired brothers and sisters. She has just completed a nursing assistant's course. Angie plans to work with the elderly in a nursing home. She has compassion and a strong love for older people.

Lisa, fifteen, was invited to California to visit her birth mother after Rachel and Bill were here. Again we hesitated and prayed before we agreed. She met her grandmother and grandfather, aunts, uncles, and cousins. They thought she was wonderful. Lisa called to tell us how much she missed us—and her horse.

We are delighted because three of our children were in Teen Missions during a recent summer. They raised their own support money, just as Jeremy did when he went to Mexico, and later to Bolivia.

Lisa is one of the three. She went to Haiti and worked with her team members on the "Feed the Hungry" program and with orphan children.

Marci, eighteen, is painfully struggling through adolescence. She is attending college to become a legal-aid secretary.

Cammi, twenty-four, married John Lucas, the son of one of my best friends, Norma Lucas, who was the originator of PLAN.

Cammi and John have had their first baby, Nicole Choe (Shay) Lucas. She is absolutely adorable!

April, twenty-five, lives at home and attends a community college. The Lord gave April a vision three years ago of ministering to her own people in Korea. One summer she and her mission team went to Korea to build a church. She was so excited about going—it meant the fulfillment of that dream.

Susan, eighteen, is enrolled in a pre-nursing program in college. She loves to read, ride horseback, and cook.

Joe, eighteen, is a senior in a Christian high school. He is considering the possibility of joining the Air Force.

Paul, sixteen, is gifted in business matters. He spent the summer with Teen Missions in Mexico. He and his team members built a Bible college.

Christina, sixteen: Life has taken a positive turn for Christina. She is happy and a blessing to her family. We see her making great strides emotionally, and we are more hopeful for her future than ever before. She is doing well in a private Christian school.

Mark, twenty-one, has graduated from McMinnville High School. The ceremony was held outside. The graduates wore red caps and gowns. Mark limped his way to the podium in front of the crowded bleachers. One by one, all the spectators in the bleachers stood to their feet, cheering and clapping for Mark.

I could not hold back the tears. It was one of my proudest moments because I knew Mark had been an inspiration not only to our family, but to the entire school and community.

Mark is now working at Mid-Valley Workshop for handicapped people. They do contract work for companies, such as assembling dental and electronic supplies. They make furniture and do other woodworking jobs. They also operate a greenhouse in Amity, Oregon.

After Mark is more established as a wage earner, he will have an opportunity to go into a semisupervised, independent apartment living program. The future looks bright for Mark.

Aaron, twelve, is in a class for trainable children in junior high. He cooperates with his teachers and works hard. He enjoys being in a Boy Scout group for handicapped children, and is in a special Olympic sports program. He leads a very fulfilled life, and proudly sweeps the floor every day.

Aaron has a sweet relationship with Jesus. He tells me, "Mama, I love Jesus. He is always with me."

He still hides and jumps out to "scare" me—and laughs. We adore Aaron and can't imagine life without him.

Maria, sixteen, continues to live with the family in Salem. She is maturing and becoming more responsible. She has one more year of high school and is thinking of becoming a nurse.

Jeremy, nineteen, is a senior in high school, and plans to enter a Christian college after graduation. He is a cook in a Chinese restaurant in the evenings. A high point for him was when he went to Bolivia with Teen Missions and helped in an orphanage. He left a piece of his heart there.

When I learned that Jeremy would be working with orphans, I bought trinkets for him to take the children. He stared when he saw that among the small gifts was a box of new pencils. I asked why. He replied, "Mom, when I was a little boy in an orphanage in Vietnam, someone came and gave us pencils. Mine was red. When I held it in my hand, I knew I could learn to write. I knew I could be somebody."

James, nineteen, lives in Portland and works in a restaurant.

John, twenty, lives in Salem. He works and attends school.

Phil and I keep busy with our large family. We now have eleven children at home. We don't know what the future will bring, but our door is open to whomever God would send.

I am still directing the adoption agency PLAN. It continues to grow. A large number of children have found homes with loving families.

We think Carlos, a nineteen-year-old boy from Bolivia, will come soon to stay with us and attend college. We are helping to support him now. His parents are Bolivian and are in the ministry in their home country.

We always seek to be sensitive to the Lord's leading and obedient to his calling. Without him nothing can be accomplished. It is our prayer that our lives will always be a testimony to God's faithfulness and love.

APPENDIX
Steps in Adopting a Child

Agencies differ in their policies and sources of children. If a family feels God has a child for them or they want to reach out to a homeless child, they should contact an adoption parent group or the state adoption service and obtain a list of their local adoption agencies. They should initially contact the local agencies to learn about their services and requirements, and the availability of children through that agency.

They should assess their needs. If adoptive parent educational classes are available, they should definitely attend, to learn all they can about the various aspects of adoption. It would be helpful to join adoptive parent support groups and develop contacts with other adoptive parents and children.

When a family feels ready, they should contact the adoption agency of their choice and proceed with the adoption process.

(1) They would make an initial application to give the agency brief information about themselves and the type of child they desire.

(2) They would meet with a social worker who would help them assess their strengths and discuss their preferences in children. The social worker would then write a report evaluating the couple's lifestyle, family backgrounds, parenting skills, and readiness for raising children. Such a report facilitates the placement of a child.

(3) Normally, one can expect a waiting period of a few months before the process of finding a child is completed.

The waiting is hard. By then a family is ready for a child, and the days seem to pass slowly. This is when they need the support of friends and relatives. They also should keep in close contact with the agency and remind themselves that the agency is as eager to place a child in an adoptive home as the family is to have the child.

The social worker is the facilitator who makes this possible.

(4) Finally the glorious day comes. The placement is made. The family receives the child with open arms.

(5) Usually at first there is a honeymoon period when the child is trying to please the parents and everyone is on his best behavior. Soon the child starts testing the parents' love. That is when the parents need to become firmer and more committed to make the adoption a success.

Sometimes the bonding process can take several years, as many children have been hurt by adults in their early lives. It takes love and patience on the part of an adoptive parent to reinstill trust into the heart of a child again. Some families need counseling to help them through this time.

Many families are so pleased by adopting that they have broadened their family circle by eventually taking in several children.

I personally feel nothing can be more rewarding than being involved in the life of a child. The Adoption Creed captures that feeling perfectly:

ADOPTION CREED

Not flesh of my flesh,
Nor bone of my bone,
But still miraculously my own.
Never forget
For a single minute,
You didn't grow
Under my heart, but in it.

—Author Unknown

Note: For anyone interested in more information regarding adoption, contact:
Plan Loving Adoptions Now
P. O. Box 667
McMinnville, OR 97128
(503:472-8452)